PASSIONATE OUTLIER

PASSIONATE OUTLIER:
GAY WRITERS AND ALLIES ON THEIR WORK

Frank Pizzoli

THE LIBRARY OF HOMOSEXUAL CONGRESS
NEW ORLEANS & NEW YORK

Published in the United States of America by
The Library of Homosexual Congress
A Rebel Satori Imprint
www.rebelsatoripress.com

Cover photo property of Frank Pizzoli

ISBN: 978-1-60864-359-2

CONTENTS

PUBLICATION HISTORY

Edmund White Discusses "Gay Culture," *Originally published in Lambda Literary Review, Summer 2007, Vol. 15, Issue 2*

Christopher Bram – Eminent Outlaws: The Gay Writers Who Changed America, *Originally published in Lambda Literary Review, July 11, 2012*

Edmund White: Invention, Imagination, and Memory *Originally published in Lambda Literary Review, March 19, 2012*

The Violet Quill: In Conversation with Surviving Members Andrew Holleran, Felice Picano & Edmund White, *Originally published in Lambda Literary Review April 10, 2013*

The Martin Duberman Reader: The Essential Historical, Biographic and Autobiographical Writings, *Originally published in Lambda Literary Review, September 1, 2013*

Sean Strub, Body Counts: A Memoir of Politics, Sex, AIDS, and Survival, *Originally published in Lambda Literary Review, January 11, 2014*

Michael Carroll: On His New Short Story Collection, the Benefits of a Spare Writing Style, and His Literary Inspirations, *Originally published in Lambda Literary Review, July 2, 2014*

John Rechy: On the Gay Sensibility, Melding Truth and Fiction, and His Literary Legacy, *Originally published in Lambda Literary Review, September 10, 2014*

Felice Picano: On Remembering the Past, the AIDS Crisis, and Gay Activism, *Originally published in Lambda Literary Review, March 11, 2015*

Michael Mewshaw Demystifies Celebrated Author in Sympathy for the Devil: Four Decades of Friendship with Gore Vidal, *Originally published in Lambda Literary Review, July 1, 2015*

Eighteen Writers Digest Christopher Isherwood's 1939 Migration to the US, *Originally published in Lambda Literary Review, April 11, 2016*

Jay Parini Discusses Gore Vidal in His Official Biography,

Originally published in Windy City Times, August 3, 2016

Susan Quinn Unravels Eleanor Roosevelt and Lorena Hickok's Love Affair, *Originally published in Windy City Times, December 12, 2016*

Equality: What Do You Think About When You Think of Equality? edited by Paul Alan Fahey, *Originally published in Lambda Literary Review, April 6, 2017*

Martin Duberman's Jews, Queers, Germans: A Novel, *Originally published in Windy City Times, June 21, 2017*

Lesbian Avenger Co-founder Anne-christine d'Adesky on ACT UP and Her Memoir, *Originally published in Lambda Literary Review, July 4, 2017*

Salman Rushdie Tackles Gender Identity in The Golden House, *Originally published in Gay & Lesbian Review Worldwide, November-December 2017*

Daniel Mendelsohn: The Odyssey Is All About Father and Son, *Originally published in Gay & Lesbian Review Worldwide, March-April 2018*

Painter Duncan Hannah Talks about His Raucous Life in 70s New York City, *Originally published in The Brooklyn Rail, May 2018*

Michael Carroll's Stella Maris and Other Key West Stories Vicious, Slippery Fun, *Originally published in Windy City Times, Sept. 17, 2019*

INTRODUCTION

I have always enjoyed asking people questions and then sharing their answers with others.

At the age of 10, I started *The Daily Blab* with my friend David and his sister Joan. We would think of a question of the day and who we might ask. To their answer we would add information drawn from an Encyclopedia Britannica and then hand-write out an issue.

A nearby mom and pop store would sell us a small ream of typewriter paper for five cents. That price is what determined how much a subscription should cost. With my grocery store owner Uncle Sauce, Joan's mother, and a neighbor on our street we were proud to have three paying subscribers. The fact that Uncle Sauce was a grocer helped. He would put the latest issue out on his counter for customers to read. When an older cousin asked how we determined the subscription price, I explained that a ream of paper cost a nickel. He laughed heartily saying, " I see you understand the law of supply and demand." I didn't but faked it, not unlike many future adult moments concerning more serious matters.

Asking people questions and recording their answers for later reporting has served me well over the years. I spent my professional life in journalism and human services. One involves reporting out what is found to be the story with all available facts known at the time of publication. Answers to human services questions were legally restricted to "a need-to-know basis." But with both endeavors the mission was the same – find out what happened and tell those who need to know all about it.

Since those childhood days I have continued my journalism, as an editor of my college newspaper and a freelance writer for a long list of newspapers and magazines nationwide, then I edited a local business journal. Eventually, in 2001, I founded *Central Voice*, an advertising-based LGBTQ bimonthly newspaper and website that lasted 20 years until Covid closed us down. We garnered 23 awards from the PA News Media Association. In recent years, I've written regularly for the nation's first alternative news weekly *The Village Voice, Brooklyn Rail, and Pennsylvania Capital-Star.*

On the human service side, accurately gathering information from people taught me the importance of making sure stories adequately reflect an individual's thoughts and feelings, not my own. When what started out being called GRID (Gay Related Immune Deficiency), later AIDS (Acquired Immune Deficiency Syndrome), and now simply HIV began rearing its ugly head, securing accurate information could literally mean the difference between life and death.

I have lived with HIV for most of my adult life, having been infected during what is called the First Wave cohort of patients. I spent two years on two different forms of chemotherapy to tamp down what my doctor described as the worst case of Kaposi's sarcoma she had ever seen. I finished with good but not conclusive results around the time that doctors began using HIV medicines in triple combinations rather than as single or double agents. I have a nondescript box that contains decades of obituaries and funeral programs for legions of gay men and others who weren't able to hang on until durable treatment protocols could be established. During those years, even now, I cannot bring myself to open it except for when I have to place yet another death notice inside.

In the 1980s with many other committed individuals, I participated in the founding of a volunteer organization that eventually became a state and federally funded HIV program. About a decade later, in 1997, when newer life-saving medicines finally began restoring lives, I founded Positive Opportunities, honored by President George H. W. Bush with a Points of Light Foundation award. The organization worked with established agencies to move HIV patients away from "I'm going to die" toward "Help me get my life back" programming. Many resumed work, a social life, and re-entered the general health care system of insurance and care. HIV was no longer a death sentence for me and millions worldwide.

As HIV increasingly manifested itself in my life, I began to write regularly for POZ magazine and virtually every other HIV trade publication spawned by the hideous disease. In 1996 and 2001, I received grants from the New York-based PEN Writers Fund for Writers & Editors. This visibility fueled my speaking at several Gay Men's Health Summits staged nationwide (1999-2002). Writing about HIV allowed me the privilege of developing a network of deeply informed readers, editors, and activists, many of them also facing the same health conditions. By 2001, I produced a regional staging of The Normal Heart by Larry Kramer, discussing with him what changed and what remained the same as "homosexuals" continued to wage their battles. With support from The Tony Cox Community Fund, The Foundation for Enhancing Communities, and Xfinity, I produced *Second Lazarus*, a documentary about living with HIV in central Pennsylvania and screened on Comcast/Xfinity and at film festivals.

Along my HIV journey, I had the opportunity to participate in the film *Positively Naked (2005)*, artist Spencer Tunick's third 'Naked' documentary celebrating *POZ* magazine's 10th anniversary. Eighty-five HIV-positive men and women gathered at Florent, the legendary 24/7 Meatpacking District bistro where we all got naked for the camera, including the owner Florent Morellet, to create an unsentimental look at life with AIDS in America. The award-winning short documentary can be found on most major content streamers. In 2021, upon the 40th anniversary of the Centers for Disease Control declaring the first AIDS case, an *ABC News Live* producer contacted me about doing a segment with Michael Gottlieb, MD, who authored the ominous report. A year later I was asked to participate in my region's Take Charge HIV media campaign for that year's World AIDS Day.

In 2010, when I was named a Living Legacy celebrating Harrisburg's 150th anniversary, I said, "Someone always comes before us. Honor them. We grow in their soil." *Out in Central Pennsylvania: The History of an LGBTQ Community* by William Burton with Barry Loveland illustrates my own work, and the work of legions of others, as we wrestled inequalities laced with erratic bouts of violence. I have been amply acknowledged and rewarded by the many kind individuals with whom I've worked over decades. I am humbled to have stood on their shoulders and learned from them.

Knowing that legions of gay men of my generation would succumb to HIV, I turned my attention to those writers of my generation who provided us with narratives of their lives. Today, younger readers can 'stand on their shoulders' by reading their interviews and books for firsthand accounts from men who lived through and survived pre- and post-Stonewall and AIDS. Remember, in 1948, homosexuality was illegal in all the Union's 48 states. Made a state in January 1959, Alaska did not declassify same-sex sexual activity until 1980. Hawaii was admitted to the Union six months after Alaska and where same-sex sexual activity has been legal there since 1973, being one of the first six states to legalize such activity. Still, as of October 1, 2023, 12 U.S. states had statutes criminalizing consensual sodomy: Florida, Georgia, Kansas, Kentucky, Louisiana, Massachusetts, Michigan, Mississippi, North Carolina, Oklahoma, South Carolina, and Texas. I suppose this is an example of "leave it up to the states," an idea that has created chaos for individuals whose behavior has been regulated one way or another in the history of this nation. And the forces of fear and hate are at it again. There is nothing consistent in how we legislate and regulate body autonomy for women, transgender individuals, and anyone declared "other." And now, after all our progress, I fear we're moving back to our former status as pariah. We're accused of 'grooming' children when mention of us is included in any school curriculum at any level. PEN America reports that 3,360 book bans were put into place in U.S. public schools and libraries in the 2022-23 school year. That's up 33% from the previous year.

Like at age 10 when I asked neighbors questions, I wanted to ask the writers who interpreted my generation's experience through their work what they thought about, well, everything – their own and others' work as well as their reflections on past and current events. Several faithful readers, one of whom knows more than one interviewee, was kind enough to share with me that it sounded to him like we were having a conversation; it didn't sound like an interview.

The book reflects pre-Stonewall times and the time between that defining event and the arrival of AIDS. Writers share their views of the past and current events, other writers, and their subjects.

The interviews and the occasional book review are presented in the order they were published, from 2007 to 2019.

We begin with Edmund White discussing "gay culture." He talks about his familiar take on gay culture as one of three horrible fates assigned to being queer – that it was a crime, a sin, or mental illness.

Next, we hear from Christopher Bram in *Eminent Outlaws: The Gay Writers Who Changed America*. He provides readers with a fifty-year survey beginning in 1948, when gay men lived under the conditions White discusses in the opening interview. We hear about the publishing industry, the state of literary fiction, and how Truman Capote, Gore Vidal, Tennessee Williams, James Baldwin, Christopher Isherwood, Allen Ginsberg, Edward Albee, Edmund White, Armistead Maupin, Mart Crowley, and Tony Kushner changed American culture. Bram argues that the gay revolution began as a literary revolution and that repression doesn't always make for good literature.

Then, we return to Edmund White who addresses the themes of *Invention, Imagination, and Memory* and how "... gays only make up about 3% of the population so we spend our whole lives 'translating' straight movies, books, ballets into gay terms and studying the heterosexuals around us..."

What follows is a Queer Trifecta. An extended interview (also available in audio form on YouTube) with Andrew Holleran, Felice Picano, and White about their heady days with The Violet Quill. They are the surviving members of the seven-member group. Between 1988 and 1990, AIDS claimed the lives of members Christopher Cox, Robert Ferro, Michael Grumley, and George Whitmore. The totality of their combined work represents a turning of the tide in gay literature for both gay readers and the publishing industry.

In November 1980, New York's *SoHo Weekly News* tagged a cover story *Fag Lit's New Royalty*, referring to the seven writers. Since the publication of that story, they have brought out the best in admirers and the worst in detractors. The auspicious group met only eight times between March 31, 1980, and March 3, 1981. They reminisce like three old friends. Their sexual affairs with each other were not unusual in New York City at the time.

Martin Duberman has the style of a public intellectual from a bygone era. In *The Martin Duberman Reader: The Essential Historical, Biographic and Autobiographical Writings*, the master historian compiles the core of his most important writings for a new generation of activists, scholars, and readers, his understandings of what has come before us, including the

Black, anti-Vietnam War, and Women's movements.

Sean Strub is linked in numerous ways to the gay civil rights movement and HIV benchmark events. His memoir, *Body Counts: A Memoir of Politics, Sex, AIDS, and Survival* is a fascinating blend of iconic moments. Yoko Ono, Warhol associates, Tennessee Williams, Gore Vidal, and all sorts of New York City royalty enter the story.

In his first collection of short stories, *Little Reef & Other Stories*, Michael Carroll employs an economy of words that describe characters deeply drawn. We've all known people like them. When reading his 12 varied tales, I thought of a sculptor who hones away clay to display what he wants us to see. That's what Carroll does. He's just writing down the way he views the world, all absurdities noted, none judged.

John Rechy's *On the Gay Sensibility, Melding Truth and Fiction, and His Literary Style* talks about his long life that bridges The Great Depression, World War II, the Korean and Vietnam War, the tumultuous 60s, the Stonewall Riots, AIDS, and the assimilation of the LGBT community into marriage and the Armed Forces. He was raised Mexican-American in El Paso, Texas at a time when Latino children were routinely segregated.

Award-winning author Felice Picano's *True Stories Too: People and Places from My Past* deals with his old New York City haunts, family, friends, and lovers – and, the legendary bookstore Rizzoli, where we hear about Salvador Dalí, Jerome Robbins, Jackie Onassis, Gregory Peck, Mick Jagger, S. J. Perelman, I. M. Pei, Philip Johnson, Josephine Baker, and John Lennon, who all shopped at the iconic bookstore when Picano worked there, providing readers intimate access to the private and cultural lives of his times.

In *Sympathy for the Devil: Four Decades of Friendship with Gore Vidal*, Michael Mewshaw deals with the light and dark sides of Vidal viewed at close range. Mewshaw and his wife, Linda, first met him in October 1975 in Rome, when Mewshaw approached Vidal to write what became a years-long series of magazine interviews revealing an individual as complex and gorgeous as any of Vidal's historical or fictional characters.

In *The American Isherwood* edited by James J. Berg and Chris Freeman, eighteen writers in essay form cover Isherwood's 1939 migration to the US, *A Single Man*, his spiritual life and relationship to Swami Prabhavananda, Isherwood's friends, Hollywood's celebrity culture, and the reception of gay-themed writing in 1960s Cold War America. The essays reveal how Isherwood used autobiographical experience in his writing as a lens to focus on the world and his times.

Jay Parini is Vidal's official biographer. *In Empire of Self: A Life of Gore Vidal*, he discusses his years-long relationship with Vidal – his biographer lineage; how Parini dealt with thin-skinned Vidal; Vidal's first love, Jimmy Trimble; and reflections on Tim Teeman's book *In Bed with Gore Vidal* and William Buckley regarding the "pedophile" slander.

Susan Quinn delves into Eleanor Roosevelt and Lorena Hickok's love affair in *Eleanor and Hick: The Love Affair That Shaped A First Lady* based on letters between Eleanor and Associated Press reporter Lorena Hickok (known as Hick). Essentially, Quinn's premise is in stark contrast to author Doris Faber's 1980 book, who was, Quinn says, "shocked" at the letters' content and left them out in her account of their relationship.

In *Equality: What Do You Think About When You Think of Equality?* edited by Paul Alan Fahey (deceased, 2017), readers are treated to 25 essays by assorted writers and everyday people interrogating the meaning of equality. Some of what is shared is based on a single experience while others weave several personal events into a pattern. All were transformative.

In *Jews, Queers, Germans: A Novel*, Martin Duberman offers a gripping account of documented history in novel form. Readers eavesdrop on Kaiser Wilhelm, Fritz Krupp, Count Harry Kessler, Walter Rathenau, and Prince Philipp of Eulenburg.

A co-founder of The Lesbian Avengers, Anne-christine d'Adesky's *The Pox Lover* addresses the legacy of 1990s radical lesbian activism, too often overshadowed by the work of gay men during that era. A pioneering American AIDS journalist, lesbian activist, and daughter of a French-Haitian family, d'Adesky's work here draws from her journals. The book careens wildly and thoughtfully, like her, from New York City to Paris, from DC to Haiti. She inventories the many lives she lived while fighting vociferously for social justice issues.

Salman Rushdie's *The Golden House* is set in New York City, opening on the day of Barack Obama's first inauguration. He speaks about a main character's struggles with gender identity, the existential choices it implies, and the situation of transgender people in India and around the world.

When Daniel Mendelsohn's 81-year-old father Jay enrolled in his seminar on *The Odyssey* at Bard College, which was followed by a Greek cruise, they experienced what Mendelsohn

10

refers to as their "own little epic." Their adventures resulted in a full-length memoir titled *An Odyssey: A Father, a Son, and an Epic*. In keeping with his hybrid style in previous works, Mendelsohn again combines the personal with the literary and the historical as he elaborates parallels between Homer's classic work and his own "odyssey" with his father.

Painter Duncan Hannah (deceased, 2022) retraces his life of endless parties and celebrity-like attention in New York City in *Twentieth-Century Boy: Notebooks of the Seventies*. He offers great detail on the gritty below 14th Street crowd and bold-faced celebrities – Allen Ginsburg, David Bowie, Andy Warhol, and the Max's Kansas City scene.

Michael Carroll's second short story collection *Stella Maris and Other Key West Stories* describes the end-of-the-line bohemian oasis that brings into its pages people from everywhere. His readers are treated to the never-ending parade of condo time share inhabitants, chain stores, and Redneck Riviera clientele. Key West is a mecca for gay men and the women who love them. His stories cover youth and age, gay and straight, the past and its prisoners, AIDS, the unpredictable nature of life, survival, new beginnings, and final recognitions.

In their interviews, several authors stressed the importance of knowing our history.

POZ magazine founder Sean Strub laments the quickening "rate at which the past is forgotten." As I was drafting my *Introduction*, I noticed in the July 2023 print edition of *Harper's* magazine that the *Readings* section started off with an excerpt from Alva Noe's *The Entanglement: How Art and Philosophy Make Us What We Are*. His book is about a young girl's dancing days and the magazine's excerpt was titled *Dancer from the Dance*. There was no mention of the fact that Andrew Holleran's iconic 1978 gay novel carries the exact same title. In the gay classic, he captures the queer movement's heady times immediately following the June 28, 1969, Stonewall Riot up until June 5, 1981, when the Centers for Disease Control declared what became known as AIDS a real threat. It was a time when our sense of liberation and equality was defined, especially by white, gay men, as primarily sexual. Our future felt limitless. Noe confirmed that *Harper's* editors selected the title.

When I brought the use of his book title to Holleran's attention, he replied in his email: "That's so odd. Either they knew they were referring to my novel or they didn't, which means the title is familiar enough to have entered public conversation without people knowing what it refers to – which I guess in a way is a compliment. But I hope you keep it in your *Introduction*, as that serves as a corrective and certainly makes Strub's point about forgetting the past. Thanks for the heads up."

If, as writers, activists, and advocates, we stand on the shoulders of all those who came before us, it is our first responsibility to know who they were in their own words. Presented here are 20 interviews and reviews in which my main endeavor was to have each participant adequately portrayed.

EDMUND WHITE DISCUSSES "GAY CULTURE"

Edmund White (born 1940) is irrepressible. By 2007, I'd devoured 20 of his 32 books. No wonder Vladimir Nabokov so generously praised his work. Susan Sontag, whom he knew well and skewered in *Caracole* (1985), thought he had his greatest influence as a cultural critic. His latest book, *The Loves of My Life: A Sex Memoir*, launches early 2025.

While White was vacationing in Key West, a mutual friend asked him to consider an interview with me. He responded by email in less than 35 minutes. We were strangers. Searching a hallway for his apartment door, White peaked out beaming a huge smile. He brewed some tea sent by friend he made in Paris. "And some dried fruit?" he asked. I felt like if I'd said, "No thanks, but how about a grilled cheese sandwich," he'd have asked how dark I'd like the bread grilled.

Setting up a tape recorder in his living room, his husband Michael Carroll scurried through with plastic baskets. "We're doing laundry today. We can wait to do that," White assured. When he finally sat down, I realized he was just as excited as I was. He only glanced at my Q&A. "I like these things to be fresh," he explained.

Fumbling with the recorder, I finally got it working. "I'm sitting here in the apartment of Edmund Wilson..." I said, and then froze with embarrassment. "We'd both be in trouble if that were true," White quipped and we both laughed. He is human despite the lacerating criticisms over time— that he's this or that; that he's not this or that; that he's not every mother's dream, as if any one of us is. We discussed pre-and post-1969/Stonewall themes, sexual liberation, art vs. "gay" art. The day before the interview, I attended the ACT UP's 20th anniversary march in New York City.

In your collection of essays, Arts and Letters you wrote "in those years long before gay liberation no one could write a proud, self-respecting, self-affirming gay text, since no gay man, no matter how clever had found a way to like himself." Can we ever expect that someone will write from a different point of view? Has that happened?

Yes, because I was really talking about before 1969. That is, I was trying to point out that people as brilliant as James Baldwin or Marcel Proust never gave a positive portrait of homosexuality at all. Although Baldwin, to be fair, tried in his last book, *Just Above My Head*, but there it had to be in the family, between two teenage, very innocent Black guys who were both musicians.

Early portrayals of homosexuality had to be heavily coded?

They're all filters. He had to go to fairly extreme measures. And anyway, that book was written long after gay liberation, so I guess my real point is that before gay liberation there really aren't that many books that show homosexuality in a positive light. *City of Night*, no. Jean Genet, no. If the three possible ideas of homosexuality were that it was a crime, a sin, or mental illness, Genet at least chose the strongest position, which is that it was a crime. Calling it a crime is a healthier point of view than saying it is a mental illness, which is the one description most middle-class people chose.

Your answer reflects what you wrote in Arts and Letters about a time "When no homosexual could defend his identity as anything other than an illness, a sin or a crime." Does that identity persist today given that suicide rates among gay teens are so high; the highest number of teenage runaways are gay teens? Critics say we fought for sexual liberation and sexual liberation only, and we ended up with AIDS.

Also, alcoholism. They say that one out of every four gays is an alcoholic. I don't know. The sexual liberation equals AIDS is, well, ridiculous. Frankly, we weren't reading a crystal ball. We had no idea what the results of the promiscuity would be. The truth is that Americans are so moralistic that they want to blame AIDS on promiscuity. But I have a very dear friend, my best friend, who died of AIDS, and he had sex only six times in his life. There is actually a dangerous aspect to all this. It's as though people think that if they have sex with just one person, or if they know their names, or just sex with three people, then they can have unsafe sex, because they are not like those sluts who are having sex with a hundred people but having safe sex. But the truth is that the person that is having sex with three people unsafely is much more at risk than the person that is having sex with 100 people using condoms. So, I would say that this whole way of linking promiscuity to AIDS is not only cruel and wrong and ahistorical, since nobody back in the late '70s-early-'80s knew that it was going to lead to AIDS. But on the other hand, for people today, it is a misleading and dangerous idea.

In **The City and the Pillar,** *Gore Vidal says about homosexuality that he wanted to show "the dead-on normalcy of it all," careful to also clarify that the book wasn't based on his life and that the characters he wrote about he didn't really know of from real life.* I haven't read the book in years, but as I recall, there's a lot of trying to get straight sailors in bed, and there's a lot of catty bitchy dialogue between the gays, which is all fine and that is interesting and was true of the period.

I certainly don't want to be an apostle for positive role models or political correctness of any sort. But I feel that what is remarkable is that no matter how intelligent the authors are, you have to wait until you get to (Christopher) Isherwood in *A Single Man* before a reader can find a picture of a guy that is just a guy. There's no one who's gay, no ideology, you don't know how he came to be that way. He has a lover that has just died, he teaches in school, he's English living in Los Angeles, and he has friends who are also English and who are straight. So, in other words it's a life like any other. And that is remarkable, that is the real breakthrough of Isherwood's book. And, of course, he published it six years before gay liberation began.

When I speculate on how Isherwood beat everybody else to

the punch, I think it's partly because he was connected to the first gay liberation of Magnus Hirschfeld in Berlin, where he lived in rented quarters next to Hirschfeld's Institute for Sexual Science. He lived in Hirschfeld's house. He has a lot of class confidence because he was upper middle-class and he lived in California, which was a kind of breeding ground for new ideas about homosexuality. All those guys who discovered they were gay in the war and who didn't go home and stayed in those beach communities in order to perpetuate some kind of freedom far from their families. That was the really beginning of the new ideas of homosexuality and, of course, they had an early gay magazine – *One* magazine.

Was it a muscle mag?
No, that was something else. That was *The Grecian Guild* or whatever. These were gay magazines that had long articles by shrinks about homosexuality and it was called *One*. It wasn't what we would consider very liberating, but the fact that it existed at all is remarkable.

And when a psychiatrist in those days would write about homosexuality it was to temper the negative?
No, it still is negative. But in those days things were so, well it's like if you were Black you were thrilled to see Stepin Fetchit in the movies because there were no other images and it was at least something, some image. So, in the same way, gays would say "Oh, now this is an important psychiatrist and he's a heterosexual and he's thinking about our problems, so we should all be very flattered." That was where they were in their

consciousness.

So, in the original admonition of Harry Hay's Mattachine Society where he suggested that activists ought to show up in clean white shirts, black ties, and their little coats, our West Coast predecessors also thought queers should present like Ozzy and Harriet?

Right, that was the idea. Because I think that the public conception was Liberace, or the idea was that you were some bleach blond working as a waiter.

What about diversity in our community? Have we achieved diversity, a frequent demand we make of others, within our own community?

I think so. For instance, recently I attended, with Larry Kramer and others from those years, the Gay Men's Health Crisis 20th Anniversary. One reason we named it "gay men's" health crisis is because we didn't want to have to deal with lesbians. At that point, 1981, there were still among gay men sore feelings about recent encounters with lesbians in any kind of political or community activity. There was still a period of lesbian separatism. There were a lot of hostile feelings. Twenty years later, at the anniversary dinner, easily half the people there were lesbians, at a dress-up dinner with Senator Hilary Clinton and Rosie O'Donnell. It was just a marvelous warm atmosphere.

How about movement versus market? Have we swallowed the media Kool-Aid on gay TV programming, Logo TV, Here TV?

Well, I think there are two things. There are officially labeled "gay culture" venues with *Logo* and a lot of the *Queer Eye* stuff. There's that, and then there are all these fascinating gay people actually making great works of art. They happen to be gay, but that is not the main burden of what they are doing. They are Michael Cunningham, Jasper Johns, or John Ashbery, or all those great ballet dancers. Lots of musicians. There are a lot of extraordinary people in the world.

Two things have been devastating to New York City and explain why New York is a lot duller a city now than it was 20 years ago. First, the cost of living in New York has driven out all the young people. You used to be able to be a waiter two nights a week, support yourself the rest of the time, and you could go to your Herbert Berkoff class and learn how to be an actor. But now, no. That's the main reason why New York is dull these days. But I think the other reason is that a lot of the really interesting gay people died off in the 1980s. I did a piece for *Art Forum* that was a tribute to a lot of people in the arts who have died, and they weren't people who made "gay art."

They made art that was well received.
Yeah, that's right. I just think of one, Scott Burton, who was a sculptor who made chairs in marble and granite and different materials. He was a famous artist in the 1980s and he was gay, he was in the leather bars every night of his life. But he never made anything "gay" that I know of.

CHRISTOPHER BRAM – *EMINENT OUTLAWS: THE GAY WRITERS WHO CHANGED AMERICA*

Christopher Bram (born 1952) has written nine novels ranging in subject matter from gay life in the 1970s to the frantic world of theater people in contemporary New York. He's written or co-written several screenplays. His 1995 novel *Father of Frankenstein,* about film director James Whale, was made into the 1998 movie *Gods and Monsters* starring Ian McKellen, Lynn Redgrave, and Brendan Fraser. Bill Condon directed and won an Academy Award for the adapted screenplay. Bram is a 2001 Guggenheim Fellow and a 2003 recipient of the Bill Whitehead Award for Lifetime Achievement.

Eminent Outlaws: The Gay Writers Who Changed America, covers a fifty-year survey of literature beginning in 1948, when homosexuality was illegal throughout the U.S., about the publishing industry, the state of literary fiction, and how Truman Capote, Gore Vidal, Tennessee Williams, James Baldwin, Christopher Isherwood, Allen Ginsberg, Edward Albee, Edmund White, Armistead Maupin, Mart Crowley, and Tony Kushner changed American culture. He included delicious biographical detail.

In a celebrity obsessed culture, it's the norm to wonder what an individual with a high profile is like one-on-one. Bram breaks the rules. In cementing details, he explained that he normally had only cold coffee to serve in his writer's office but offered to have some bottled water of my choice on hand. His office was modest, on the seventh floor of a larger, shared space. His ancient computer sported a tower and television-size display screen with a big rear end that said "practical." A full bookcase, a frumpy couch under the single window with a cockeyed window shade with loopy pull chords, and a low table for storing computer disks serves his purpose. A *Gods and Monsters* movie poster on one wall near his desk completed the scene. He also said he'd remember to shave the day of our interview since I'd be taking his photograph. He didn't remember. He was as three-dimensional as any of his characters are in everyday situations.

∽ ⁀ꜩ

The opening sentence of **Eminent Outlaws: The Gay Writers Who Changed America** *is that the gay revolution began as a literary revolution. Is that because publishing makes one visible?*
That's part of it, part of the bigger picture. In 1948, when the book begins, homosexuality was illegal in all 48 states. You couldn't even talk about it. Then right after World War II, a few writers started telling stories about it, fictional accounts because if they had told true stories they'd be open to prosecution, charged with committing crimes. But because they were telling fictional stories about homosexuality, they could get away with it, first in novels, then in plays, and poetry. Because writers were able to talk about homosexuality, critics could talk about it too, usually negatively, but people *were* talking about it. These

early reviews were often poisonous. It was appalling to read them right up into the early 1970s. But talk created openness, which led to more books and more talk. And the attacks began to soften. Let's not forget about that great quote attributed to Gandhi: "First they ignore you, then they make fun of you, then they attack you, and then you win." Gay books and plays were the target for a lot of the early mockery and attacks.

In **Eminent Outlaws**, *you place a particular focus on the celebrity personas of post-World War II Gore Vidal, and then Stonewall-forward Edmund White. John Leland, in his* **New York Times** *review, criticized you for not including many pop and/or outlier gay writers: James Purdy, Reynolds Price, Dennis Cooper or Augusten Burroughs, David Sedaris. What are your thoughts on Leland's critique?*

Well, as I say in my Introduction, this book is not meant to be an encyclopedia of all gay writers. I'm just doing a dozen or so writers that enable me to follow the major plotlines of a 50-year period. I'm covering a lot of territory. I did not want to write an index-card literary history, so people were inevitably left out. I'm puzzled by some of the names Leland mentions. I mean, Reynolds Price? I've actually read quite a bit of Price: he was kind of closeted. He finally wrote about gay relationships in *The Source of Light* in the 1980s. He was very coy with a main character who is in love with both a woman and one of his students. He plays the game of "Which will he choose" for 400 pages. I can't even remember if he goes for the guy or the girl at the end. It gets awfully tiresome. Leland was just trying to show off; he wanted to show off how much he knew. It's easier to talk about what's not in a book than what's in it.

Leland also, in his review, opines that although you connect the emergence of more openly gay literature to the 60s African-American Civil Rights Movements and the Anti-War Movements, you – his word – "curiously," do not connect the emerging gay sexual revolution to the broader sexual revolution of that same period. Jean Carlomusto presents in her documentary film, Sex in an Epidemic, *what I call a clarifying delineation that weaves those parallel gay and straight sexual shifts together, but they actually took place separately. I mean, straight Plato's Retreat and gay The Everard Baths and all the exclusively gay, straight, or mixed crowd discos came after those venues. Was that part of your thinking in not combining these social phenomena because those Zeitgeists didn't talk to each other initially?*

Well, this is a literary history. I'm not covering the entire gay movement. But I do talk about the sexual revolution. First indirectly, when I discuss the loosening of censorship for both gay and straight writers after the war – suddenly people were able to write about real sex. Then I address the connection directly when I talk about the coming of AIDS. I have a whole page describing the sexual revolution and its connection to the gay sexual revolution.

To tell the truth, I don't think Leland really read my book, not cover to cover the way most people read. I think he just read the jacket copy, then flipped through the index to see if I included the things he thought were important.

Do you think he perused it?

He perused it. I mean, he made so many complaints about things that I actually answer. At one point he complains that I don't talk about women. I address that in the Introduction, saying I reluctantly decided to do only the men because the story was complicated enough. The women have their own narrative, and I don't feel qualified to write it. So no, I really don't think he read the book.

You mentioned that authors couldn't write about sex – straight or gay – before World War II. Then came John O'Hara's sex romp **A Rage to Live** *(1949, 1965 movie), which is about my adopted hometown of Harrisburg, PA. His title always cracks me up because I can't imagine anybody in south central Pennsylvania having a rage for anything, let alone living.*

In the period after World War II, publishers suddenly found that sex sold. Think about those paperback post-war novels with sexy covers. Even Flannery O'Connor's books had half-naked women on the cover. Publishers found that gay sex sold too, but then backed away from it, the mainstream houses anyway. The paperback pulp houses picked it up, however, and the smaller presses.

If the general culture was homophobic, how did Gore Vidal sell **The City and the Pillar?**

It wasn't homophobic, not at first. There was a window of curiosity for three or four years when mainstream publishers were willing to explore.

The most amazing story I stumbled upon was that Vidal wrote *The City and the Pillar*, in part, because he told a straight editor over drinks about "these men" he'd been noticing around town. The editor, who didn't know Vidal was gay, encouraged Vidal to write a novel about "these men." He thought it would turn out to be a hot subject.

Your book focuses on writers who broke the long, deafening silence which changed the fabric of America. Your manuscript is added to their narrative. How did you organize Eminent Outlaws?

I would find a story thread, follow it, see where it would lead me, often to another thread and then another and another. I did not have to make up the funny lines. My subjects provided me with the best lines. If I couldn't find something, however, I couldn't make it up. I had to admit I didn't know or skip over or research or find some connection. And I was dealing with a much larger cast of characters than I usually deal with in a novel, although I do like writing ensemble novels. I've written several novels which have half a dozen major characters. This time I had a dozen and I had to wait and see what emotional drama would arise naturally out of the material.

So, if you reached a dead end, you struck it from the timeline or moved on?

Yes, but often the threads took me places I hadn't planned on going to in advance. I hate to admit it but, in my original proposal, I did not include Christopher Isherwood. But I followed Gore Vidal to Hollywood, and he met Isherwood, and the older writer became a major piece of the story. He's one of my favorite characters in the book.

And Vidal met Isherwood after The City and the Pillar *and his* after his Edgar Box period, *the mystery novels he wrote under that name to make money since he'd been shunned.*

I had to do a flashback, in effect, to Isherwood's *Goodbye to Berlin* period. (These are the stories that later became the 1951 play and 1955 film *I Am a Camera*, both starring Julie Harris, then the 1966 Broadway musical *Cabaret* and same-name 1972 film with Liza Minnelli.) Then came books that didn't quite work, like *The World in the Evening* (1954), followed by the great work: *Down There on a Visit* (1962) and *A Single Man* (1964). Except for *The Berlin Stories*, his best work came after he met Vidal.

In following those threads, you demystified Vidal for me. I've read yards of his work, admire him greatly, but don't think I'd like him as a person.

Well, when you don't treat him as timeless but watch his life unfold, Vidal becomes more human. I've been reading him since I was a teenager in the 60s and loved reading him, especially his essays. But I realized early that he wouldn't be the kind of guy I'd want to hang out with.

But unquestionably, his essays are astounding commentary, and the syntax, the synthesis of events and thought.

And we get to see a positive side of him in his essays. We know Vidal is curmudgeonly and he hates everybody; he sure hated

Truman Capote. But he loved Tennessee Williams. His two essays about Williams are wonderful appreciations of him as both a man and an artist. His essay about Isherwood is quite wonderful too. He wrote a terrific early essay about John Horne Burns, author of *The Gallery*. He could love as well as hate, which we forget.

It's difficult to accept the reality of one of our heroes being imperfect, as we all are, that Vidal and Capote could they have carried on like they did.... Perhaps Vidal was worried about Capote surpassing his **The City and the Pillar** *with his release of* **Other Voices, Other Rooms,** *at the time called "Other Vices, Other Rooms" by detractors?*

Released a week apart. And Capote was getting a lot more attention than Vidal. As I say in the book, Vidal admitted it was hard, that Capote came to literature more naturally than he did. Vidal had to work at it. Capote was kind of an idiot savant in a way. He was not terribly scholarly, unlike Vidal who was, who read a lot, whereas Capote seemed to have some natural gift that Vidal didn't have. Vidal needed to work at it; he resented Capote who didn't. Vidal knew he was smarter than Capote, but sometimes Capote could just naturally write really well.

Maybe early on, Vidal's style suffered a rigid streak from having read so much from the **Congressional Record** *to his blind grandfather, Senator Gore?*

Yes. But later he was more industrious, a very hard worker, constantly writing, not just novels, but screenplays, journalism, and he was constantly reading.

Not wanting to ever be dependent again on a bad review or being shut out, so he went to Hollywood to make money, holding his creative noise?

Yes. And also helping Vidal get over Capote and those Hollywood years was his partner, Howard Austen. He had this man in his life who, even though they never had sex, and Vidal proudly confessed that, they were still very supportive of each other. He was an anchor for Vidal; he kept him on an even keel.

Austen, whom Vidal advised to change his Jewish name from Auster in order to get hired in a bigoted New York advertising world, was kept him very well hidden by Vidal...

Vidal didn't hide Austen, but he never talked about him in print. The relationship finally came up in the *Gay Sunshine* interview when John Mitzel asked Vidal who he was going to leave his money to. Later Armistead Maupin interviewed Christopher Isherwood and Don Bacardi and they mentioned Vidal and Austen, asking why Gore never mentions Howard: "They are as much a couple as we are." So, acknowledging his relationship with Austen happened late. Only after Austen died did we see how important he really was to Vidal. He seemed lost without him.

Vidal wrote about Austen's death, returning to Los Angeles for medical care, and opened that door for readers, down to their last moments together...

That's the best portion in *Point to Point Navigation*, his account of Austen's death.

Are you working on anything right now you'd like readers to know about?

No. Just kind of exploring a couple of possibilities. I'd like to do another non-fiction book. I really enjoyed writing *Eminent Outlaws* because it uses a different side of my brain, but an emphasis on story and character.

Is there a second **Eminent Outlaws** *ahead?*

I don't know. It's too soon. Where the book ends right now is a time of transition, and I don't know what the next volume would be. If there's another Edmund White type figure to start up the narrative. I don't think there is. In a way, White is almost like the last man of letters. He's a look back to another era, but people used to say that about Edmund Wilson, and we've seen other men of letters since.

With the release of **Eminent Outlaws,** *you shared with* **The Week** *what you called six groundbreaking works by gay authors. With the exception of Gore Vidal's essay collection, your list focuses on relationships. Philip Gambone wrote in* **Something Inside: Conversations with Gay Fiction Writers,** *that your fiction is psychological and emotional. He says you find interesting material in the lives of ordinary gay people. You've discovered yourself, your homosexuality, through reading about others in gay relationships. Do relationships fuel your creative engine?*

Relationships are the most interesting thing to write about. But there's all kinds of relationships: lovers, families, friends, even enemies. It's hard to kind of come up with fiction that isn't about a relationship. Even with Robinson Crusoe, what we remember is the second half when Friday shows up, not so much the time when he's alone.

John Irving's new novel, **In One Person,** *resembles through a different lens John Weir's* **What I Did Wrong,** *where they're not changing places in the bedroom, but nobody has any trouble with anybody else's sexuality. Perhaps there is a new relationship sensibility emerging?*
I think the straight writers have recognized gayness is a great subject and they want to explore it too. I think straight readers are a little less comfortable with it, but the writers say, "I want to write about this too." The most famous example is Annie Proulx and *Brokeback Mountain.* She recognized this is a great subject and wrote about it. Indian writer, Bharati Mukherjee, in her *Desirable Daughters,* has a terrific story about three Indian sisters and who go back and forth between the United States and India, and there are two, not one, but two gay characters in it, two men who turn out to be gay, and it makes perfect sense. A short story writer and novelist, Charles Baxter, now and then he will have kind of like gay characters show up in ways that again make sense. He realizes this is part of life. I find it very exciting.

And there were writers who were not out for many years and then came out and themselves wrote about homosexuality?
I remember reading John Cheever and not knowing he was gay. When I found him writing about homosexuality in *Wapshot Chronicle* and *Falconer,* I thought, of course, it's a great subject.

And then, years later, after he dies, we find out he was bisexual. But now there are writers who we know are straight, but they recognize gay life is great material.

All this is sounding post-gay in that homosexuality in and of itself is no longer much of a drawing point unless it meaningfully connects with other aspects of a character's life or a storyline, a through-line that holds readers' interest, gay or straight?
It's not just a post-gay dilemma. It's fiction that's in trouble right now, not just gay fiction, all fiction is going through a wobbly period. I think straight novelists are having as much trouble too. There are certain genres that are in better shape than others, but I think literary fiction in particular is going through a kind of sticky place right now. Gay has always been like this box people wanted to get out of, and as I was saying earlier, in a way Gore Vidal was. He was pushing post-gay back when he said there's no such thing as a homosexual person, only a homosexual act.

Literature is not the same as athletics. Those who pass the book contract finish line first may not be running with the best manuscript under their arm. Were you making a statement about when these works of literature occurred and what was happening in the cultural and political Zeitgeist? I mean the differences in acceptance of homosexuality in the years between The City and the Pillar *and* A Boy's Own Story *are tremendous.*
Literary quality is important but it's not really the most important thing for why a book matters, why a book hits. I mean I had big problems with the writing in *The City and the Pillar*, even *A Boy's Own Story*, and Larry Kramer's *Faggots*,

and I talk about that but make clear they are still important books. There are other books I prefer more. Vidal became a much better writer than he was when he wrote *The City and the Pillar*, but it has a certain raw power that makes it important and keeps it important.

Speaking of first times, there was an initial period in gay literature, say the 70s and 80s, when anything "gay" got published. Do you think a lot of really awful manuscripts ended up on shelves in bookstores?
But a lot of good stuff did too. It's hard to say what's going to hit and what's not. I think what got published in that initial round in the 80s and early 90s – and remember, it was still hard to get a novel published – was brought to market because the publishing industry was much more open to gay material than they'd been before, or they had been recently. Some so-so books got published too but look at straight literature. There's how many just so-so too mediocre to just outright-bad books getting published? So, with increased numbers, more books on the whole being published meant that more good *and* bad books entered the market.

So not that we would hold our community to a different or higher standard. We basically joined the world of publishing.
Yes. That's how it works.

On how it works with selling books, I want to ask you this because Edmund White had mentioned, and I don't mean this as a rude question, he noted you said to him you weren't sure that publishers were interested in "gay fiction," meaning that it would be more difficult for you, and others, to actually sell those kinds of manuscripts?

Well, what has changed, it's not just gay fiction, it's all mid-list fiction. It's literary fiction. And in the past five to ten years, publishers have grown less confident. They don't believe in mid-list books anymore, and gay books are mid-list, meaning they're not going to become best sellers. In the golden age of gay literature, if you want to call it that, from the mid-70s to the mid-90s, a gay book could sell 5,000 copies in hardcover and be considered a big success and make a nice profit. That's unthinkable for publishers now. They do not know how to make enough money off of sales figures that are reasonable, but not low.

So, if we take the old book formula of a book costing $25 with $15 of it paying back investment and $5 each for author and publisher to re-invest back into midlist, that's over?

Yes, pretty much over. I think the problem for gay fiction right now is that the mainstream houses aren't sure what will sell – period. Not just gay books, but other books. However, the slack in gay titles is now being taken up by smaller houses. We're back to the early 50s when paperback lines and little presses like Greenberg handled gay books. Nowadays we have Cleis, Chelsea Station Editions, and the new Magnus Books by Don Weise.

In other words, smaller houses could run with titles longer while waiting for a return not based on quarterly numbers or a two-

week splash to prove oneself in book chains?
They paid low advances, and they could still make a profit.
Publishing now has taken Hollywood as their model, which
means huge advances, huge publicity and you must have a great
opening, or you're lost.

Like a movie making back investment in one or two weekends?
All the investors want the first dollar back in the first four days…
and right now the reading market is going through a transition.
People aren't buying books the way they used to. My theory is
because of the transition from books to E-books. They want to
read what they already own in wood pulp, what they've already
invested in, and therefore don't buy new titles – that's just my
theory and don't know if it's true.

*Regarding what sells, what doesn't, regardless of topic or genre,
there's David Bergman's book* The Violet Hour *which addresses
The Violet Quill, a group of seven white men held up as the
icons of gay publishing from that heady era between Stonewall
and the advent of AIDS. Three of them remain alive: Edmund
White, Andrew Holleran, Felice Picano. Four unfortunately are
not with us in person – Christopher Cox, Robert Ferro, Michael
Grumley, George Whitmore. All seven met only seven times
over the period of a year and they set into motion what many
call the gay literary movement. Some argue it was not a literary
movement. You say in* Eminent Outlaws *you're not sure that
it was as significant as perhaps it is, was looked upon then or
even looked upon now. Edmund White said in my last interview
with him that they used those meetings partly to "divide up turf."*

Ferro got family, White got childhood, Holleran got New York and Fire Island, and so on. That wasn't the only thing that he said about that period. What are your thoughts on the group?

Well, I see The Violet Quill as a myth. They were seven friends who met only a few times. Two of them are undeniably great writers – Edmund White and Andrew Holleran, and each did important work before they met. They continue to do important work. Three of the writers died before they could make a strong mark: Robert Ferro, George Whitmore, and Michael Grumley. George Whitmore did some terrific stuff, but then he died of AIDS. Christopher Cox did some good work before he died, but only as an editor. Felice Picano made his big breakthrough later, with *Like People in History*.

The Violet Quill was six good writers (Christopher Cox wrote very little) who did good work, but they were not the only game in town at this time. A lot of other good writers were doing terrific work too: Armistead Maupin, Larry Kramer, David Plante, and Harvey Fierstein. Christopher Isherwood was still working during this period. David Leavitt broke through in 1984. So, the Quill was a small part of a larger crowd. They were important as individuals, not as a group.

The myth of the group attracts many of us simply because writing is such a solitary activity. We love the idea of a group of writers working together. The truth of the matter is that all writers have their own little support communities, friends with whom we share ideas and encouragement. But none are as famous as the Violet Quill.

Gay is no longer exclusively defined as white, educated, effusively cultural, exclusively homosexual, an ever-expanding definition of queer. When you look at Lambda Literary Review, *the annual awards, works that are selling, there's a lot of sub-genre smash-ups of race, economic class, HIV status, disability, sex, gender. Are these current writers, same as Quill writers, all white, all male, providing readers with exactly the same source of comfort as those men did? Creating visibility?*

Yes, they're providing the same as an earlier generation of gay writers. There's some really wonderful stuff. I was just rereading poems by a terrific Puerto Rican poet, Emanuel Xavier. His *Pier Queen* collection was just reissued – it was originally published in the 90s. It's verbal snapshots of a population we usually don't hear about, mostly Black and Hispanic kids who hung out at the piers in the West Village.

As I remember from those days, they would get off that last stop on Christopher Street, by the Lucille Lortel Theater which has lots of gay theater names in stars on the pavement, go down to the pier at the street…Christopher Street was then what Chelsea is today…

At Christopher Street, yes. Xavier's poems were really strong when they first came out, but now they seem even better. They function as both history and literature. But there are other writers like Xavier telling new stories, stories that we haven't heard before. There's Rakesh Satyal, an Indian writer who did a terrific book called *Blue Boy*, about a young Indian American boy in Cincinnati, Ohio, White's hometown, an Indian American boy's own story. It's a coming-of-age novel about his double identity as both a gay kid and an Indian kid. James Hannaham a couple of years ago did an interesting book called *God Says No* about a born-again African-American gay kid, who is a real fuck-up. It's very funny and very painful. There are all these great stories still to tell that haven't been told yet.

In his interview with Richard Canning, Gary Indiana says that gay people are no longer a clandestine aristocracy and that with no secrecy there's no sensibility either. Does oppression, repression make for good art, or is Indiana reflecting on his own period?

I find that a myth too, that things were better in the Little Orphan Annie Secret Decoder Ring Society age – to steal a line from Pat Bond in the documentary *Word is Out*. We can be nostalgic about those times: Oh yes, we were all in it together and we all loved Judy Garland...

I don't remember that, at least it wasn't everyone. You?

I don't remember that either. I remember people who enjoyed Garland and musical theater, opera, but it wasn't everyone. I'm a middle-class kid from Virginia, so the idea of aristocracy doesn't appeal to me. But I don't remember any gay aristocrats, clandestine or otherwise.

And early in the 50-year period covered in Eminent Outlaws *lots of men were not returning home after World War II, instead settling here in New York City, and meeting each other away from the playful but confining Armed Forces. Some observers have described the war as the largest forced collectivization of men in history. If there was ever a period in the 20th Century where men were going to find each other, it was going to be while at war?*

Yes, yes. Allan Berube talks about that in *Coming Out Under Fire*; just suddenly all these men and gay women too, were suddenly thrown together and meeting each other.

In his interview with Richard Kenney, Colm Toibin says that gay liberation is like Northern Ireland, once the troubles are over, the novelists have a different story to tell, one which isn't as intrinsically dramatic. Yet the stories told by poet Emanuel Xavier are just as vital to readers as were earlier stories written for an all-white, male caste of homosexuals.

The world outside has changed, but you still have to "come out" and enter into that world, and doing so remains a very private, often still difficult, experience, even now in 2012.

With all these shifts in not only gay publishing but politics too, are we at a tipping point?

It's amazing in just the last couple of years – last June with New York State approving marriage equality and Obama coming out on the issue – that's quite amazing, really wonderful.

You know, there was a period when New York City was very different than it is now, when it was about the creative work, it was certainly more affordable. Fran Leibowitz has said of Interview *readers that they all knew each other. Creative people wanted to be around each other.*

They still want to be around each other. I don't think that has diminished. But they don't meet in bars and cafes in Manhattan, but out in Greenpoint and Bushwick or on the internet or through online literary blogs and magazines. There might be less public literary life in the places we expect to see it, but it's still going on, dispersed not just into other boroughs but through the whole country. You just have to look for it a little harder.

EDMUND WHITE: INVENTION, IMAGINATION, AND MEMORY

Often steeped in controversy, Edmund White remains unabridged. My second interview with him covers critics' reactions to his work after he had been criticized by the *Los Angeles Review of Books* for his work not being "universal," a barb also issued by Daniel Mendelsohn in the pages of *The New York Review of Books*, where they both have a byline.

Alas, other bold faced authors at the time toasted White. About *Jack Holmes,* White's novel out at the time of this interview, Martin Amis wrote in the *London Sunday Times* the book reveals "startling perceptions of American society... as character after character is delicately and colorfully rendered and one social milieu after another brought vividly to life. White is a connoisseur of the nuances of personality and mood, and here unveils his very human cast in all their radical individuality." The LST reviewer Edmund Gordon wrote that the novel is "a triumphant return to form...his best yet."

Upon release of *A Boy's Own Story,* French critics credited him with a "Proustian sensibility," comparing his prose to Henry James. *Paris Review* interviewer Jordan Elgrably thought his highest good "is the truth of the imagination." William Goldstein wrote in *Publishers Weekly,* "To call Edmund White merely a gay writer is to oversimplify his work and his intentions."

John Irving (*The World According to Garp, Cider House Rules*) calls him "one of the best writers of my generation." The same-age as White, Irving has said about *A Boy's Own Story* that when he first read it in the early 1980s he "thought that the novel spoke much more to me about a boy coming of age (even though it's about a gay boy coming of age, and I'm not gay) than J. D. Salinger's *The Catcher in the Rye* ever did."

~⁓⁓

In his review of City Boy: Life in New York During the 1960s and '70s, *Daniel Mendelsohn writes in* The New York Review of Books *"What's most pressingly at stake for him (White), in writing ostensibly about arts and letters, is the artists and the lettres, the social and personal aspect of literary production." What's wrong with focusing on the social and personal aspects of literary production?*
I believe that the fame of an artist or writer is mostly due to his legend, rather than his work. Look at Van Gogh, Rimbaud, Hemingway, Gertrude Stein. If we're honest about it, most of us respond to the extra-artistic image these people have. As a writer of biographies (*Proust, Genet, Rimbaud*), I'm obviously interested in their life as well as the work.

How does this idea play into the work you produce? Regarding your forthrightness in writing about your own life, warts and all? Do you find this has contributed to your own fame?
I never think about that.

"Universalism" is a blessing and a curse. Your work has just been criticized by the Los Angeles Review of Books *for not being universal. Using your interaction in* City Boy *with then-Raritan editor Richard Poirier as an example, Poirier became "furious" for your suggesting that there may be "gay" fiction, poetry, even a gay sensibility. Also, critic Daniel Mendelsohn underscores Poirier's reaction to you as you wrote it: "a betrayal of every humane idea of literature." Pretty stiff indictment?*

I'm so bored and offended by that objection. They wouldn't dare criticize a Black or Jewish writer in the same way.

Mendelsohn didn't read my pages very carefully, because at the end of the discussion I concede that I now largely agree with Poirier, though at the time I thought he was ignoring an exciting new possibility in art. In the intervening years there certainly have been many splendid gay novels and gay literary studies.

I suppose the more specific the writing is the more it intrigues the general reader. I just finished a splendid memoir, *What to Look for in Winter* by Candia McWilliam, who is a Scottish aristocrat and novelist who has gone blind and faced two unsuccessful marriages. In no way does her story parallel mine, but I identified with every page.

Readers and playgoers like a work that explores all the codes and systems of a particular world – that's why paranoia is such a good starting point for a novel (*Pale Fire*). Or why *Moby Dick* is so compelling.

Like every writer, I hope that my work will eventually reach a large audience. In the 19th century it mattered desperately whether one was a Romantic, Realist or Naturalist but now we read with equal interest Hugo, Balzac, Flaubert and Zola.

Daniel Mendelsohn has criticized A Boy's Own Story *because he feels that in the manuscript "life" overtook "art." What's wrong with that? Isn't the 20th century full of exclamations and warnings that art reflects life, that life reflects art, and now with reality TV, who can know?*

Actually, *A Boy's Own Story* only loosely echoes my own life. I was precocious intellectually and sexually, won prizes, published stories and poems and slept with 500 people before I was sixteen – quite unlike the shy, unbrilliant boy in my book.

Is there a gay sensibility? At moments, Mendelsohn sounds like a White Colonialist scolding indiginous for not acquiescing that he knows better than they, and everyone else, what's good, what's not.

I never read the Mendelsohn article, so I have no idea what he says; my partner warned me off it, since hateful criticism has a way of searing itself into my brain. I don't think there is one gay sensibility any more than there is a single Black or Jewish sensibility.

Speaking of "gay sensibility," was it a struggle to inhabit a straight male voice in your current novel Jack Holmes & His Friend?

Not at all. After all, gays only make up about 3% of the population so we spend our whole lives "translating" straight movies, books, ballets into gay terms and studying the heterosexuals around us – we know much more about them than they know about us, just as Blacks know a lot about whites but whites know virtually nothing about Blacks.

I think this is the first time you have inhabited a straight male voice.
Fiction is an accumulation of little true facts that are made dynamic – it's always an exciting challenge to pull that off.

You're good friends with John Irving and now he's featuring a lead bisexual male character in his next novel. Coincidence?
One due more to the fact that his grandfather was a cross-dresser who often appeared in amateur theatricals as a woman, and that his own son is gay (Since this interview, Irving's son, his third and youngest child is now Eva Everett Irving, a trans woman, a writer herself, and an actor and director who played Mariel in the CBC series *Sort Of*.)

You admire both Alan Hollinghurst and E. M. Forster, one writing as an openly gay man, one not. Might Forster's work have been different had he been "out"?
Of course, Forster did write a gay book, *Maurice*, except he wouldn't let it be published in his lifetime. Proust wrote a lot about homosexuality but not his own. The narrator is one of the few characters who stays straight till the end. Gays in the past, like Proust, had to be inventive and imaginative and have excellent memories, because they were always transforming

their lovers from Phil to Phyllis. Invention and imagination and memory are all good tools for a novelist.

Help us understand The Violet Quill. Looking back, the group – Christopher Cox, Robert Ferro, Michael Grumley, Andrew Holleran, Felice Picano, Edmund White, and George Whitmore – met only seven times over one year but set into motion a literary movement. As you've said: The gay community was despised in the 50s, liberated in the 60s, partied large across urban settings in the 70s, and started dying off in the 80s. Did the "Quill" chime history's clock at just the right moment?

We were enabled by the invention of new gay publications such as "Christopher Street" and about 70 new gay bookstores across the country (now sadly shuttered). We were suddenly writing fiction that addressed the gay reader, not the straight one, and that did not provide an explanation of where Fire Island was or how our characters came to be gay. We used those meetings partly to divide up the turf – Ferro got the family, I got childhood, Holleran got New York and Fire Island, et cetera.

This month in Melbourne (Feb. 2012) there's an international conference "After Homosexual: The Legacy of Gay Liberation." Not long before his death you spoke on camera with significant Off-Off Broadway principal Doric Wilson, of Caffe Cino fame. Both of you lamented the arrival of "assimilation." Are we approaching post-gay?

Post-gay has long been with us – think of Michael Cunningham's books. I regret the passing of a bohemian, Leftist gay life that was accepting of all outsiders, the mixed gay couple, the

homeless old lady. You used to see all these people in gay bars –
now they're all frightfully exclusive.

In a 1988 interview for The Paris Review *with Jordan
Elgrably, the same year* The Beautiful Room Is Empty *was
published, you note the difference between being a journalist and
a novelist and being a typical New Yorker in that you had a
keen eye for the publishing market. Yet you became discouraged
with that constant drumbeat and wrote* Forgetting Elena, *your
first published novel and one you wrote to please yourself, not a
potential market. In your more recent work, have you been able
to balance all those competing forces?*
Of course, writers in this difficult world are very aware of the
market, since even established authors have trouble getting
published; recently Christopher Bram said he wrote *Eminent
Outlaws* because he wasn't sure he could find a home for his
fiction. The theme of a novel now must be obvious and striking,
even in a quick summary.

*Andre Gide said that with each book a writer should lose the
admirers he gained with the previous one. Are you losing
admirers along the way?*
Surely.

*For what reasons may you be losing readers? And on the flipside
do you feel you gained some admirers? What does this new
audience look like?*
Some gay readers resented the amount of straight sex in *Jack
Holmes*, just as they disliked a "straight" novel such as *Caracole*,

which some gay bookstores refused to handle.

You've said that each good novel should advance a theory of the novel. Still believe that?
Yes, for instance, *Jack Holmes* uses a scenic technique I've never explored before of action and dialogue and less description and analysis than in my previous books – the Richard Yates approach, you might say.

Referring to The Beautiful Room Is Empty, *what did you mean by saying you wanted to show the puritanical oppression of sexual freedom? How is sexual freedom oppressive?*
I mean that sexual freedom is oppressed in our country, not that sex is oppressive. Sorry about the confusion. I recognize that passion is usually a destructive force; I agree with Racine, Shakespeare, Flaubert and Tolstoy.

Does your current novel Jack Holmes & His Friend *reflect that same sentiment about love and passion?*
No, my characters are not tragic.

You've said your unpublished novels written in the 50s and 60s gather dust, although you have mined them for future works. About the tone of those earlier works you've said, "In the 60s we harbored utopian notions that were extremely naïve." What utopian, naïve notions does the gay community hold today? That all of us want to get married? Have kids? Serve in the military? Be a jock? Or is the quilt picture of our community simply more complete these days?

Many gays think that if only they could have all the freedoms that straights enjoy, they'd be happy – which seems naïve.

You participated in the 1969 Stonewall Riots, which you considered a rather silly event at the time, calling it more Dada than Bastille. Is the gay liberation movement still more Dada than Bastille? Younger activist groups, like Get Equal, are storming the Human Rights Campaign offices like the Bastille.
I'm afraid the gay community these days is very corporate and serious.

You've said about yourself: "I keep feeling I've accomplished nothing, never written a 'real' novel." That was 1988 when you, and gay men everywhere, were struggling intensely with the unreality of AIDS, the fast, sequential loss of friends. Still feel that way?
I feel that *Jack Holmes* is my first "real" novel in that it is a page turner, has action and dialogue and evokes duration as well as time passing – all the hallmarks of a real novel.

And, finally, with every good sentiment in mind, how has, if at all, your recent stroke affected your thoughts about writing in general, your writing, your view of the world?
Everything seems to be conspiring to make me simplify, simplify. The stroke only exacerbated that tendency.

Research assistance provided by Shaun Espenshade.

THE VIOLET QUILL: IN CONVERSATION WITH SURVIVING MEMBERS ANDREW HOLLERAN, FELICE PICANO & EDMUND WHITE

In November 1980, New York's *SoHo Weekly News* tagged a cover story *Fag Lit's New Royalty*, referring to Andrew Holleran (born 1944), Felice Picano (born 1944), and Edmund White (born 1940), all three alive today, and Christopher Cox, Michael Grumley, Robert Ferro, and George Whitmore, who have died. Since the publication of that story, which was subtitled *A Moveable Brunch – A Fag Lit Mafia*, they have brought out the best in admirers and the worst in detractors.

In this interview, the three writers reflect on their early gay years, their time together as the Violet Quill, Grindr, writing and publishing today, writing gay characters, Queer Theory, and controversies still with us as the LGBT demographic evolves into ever-expanding, not yet fully complete diversity, including reflections on the AIDS epidemic and how it is now viewed or forgotten.

Corralling the three required a trail of emails with Holleran finally conceding "I won't be the spoiler if Ed and Felice want to, but my gut feeling is that this is a turkey that has been eaten, deboned, and already used for soup! i.e., I can't think of

49

anything that could be said that hasn't been – in fact, I rather agree with Chris Bram's estimation, in your interview with him, which I enjoyed but what do the others think?" They thought a lot over the years and this interview represents about one-third of the 30,000-plus words in our transcript.

Felice Picano and Edmund White, why did you encourage David Bergman, who wrote The Violet Hour *(2004), to continue what George Stambolian began regarding the seven-member writing group known as* The Violet Quill*?*

Picano: Like most academics, Bergman was looking for a good topic. Stambolian was friendly with all of us, and he had opened up the subject of gay male literature available to academics and Bergman.

White: I think Bergman very kindly wanted to write about this subject and not exactly a popular one. Most academics chose "Queers of the Renaissance" or something. Almost none of them wrote about contemporary writers. And Bergman is not just an academic; he's a very good writer and poet.

Holleran: Bergman's work reflected part of what is called gay publishing in the late 70s. The trend encouraged a lot of librarians, academics, who suddenly had a chance to be gay in their work.

White: We're not very written about. It's actually been a

scandalously neglected movement, I think. At Princeton where I teach the talks are mostly about Milton or Spencer, but almost nothing on gay literature of the late 20th century and forward. Even gay academics are really only interested up until about 1910.

Picano: Being alive is definitely a disadvantage.

Holleran: So, Bergman did us an enormous favor. Without him, we wouldn't be talking today.

Stephen Holden wrote in his **New York Times** *review of Robert Chelsey's play* Jerker *(1986) that "more bluntly than any other play dealing with AIDS* (Jerker) *showed how the epidemic has threatened one of the fundamental reasons for an entire community's very existence – its freedom of erotic expression – and challenged its hard-won self-esteem." What do each of you think when looking back on how sexual liberation was the Zeitgeist that drove all other energies?*

Picano: It *was* gay liberation. It *was* sexual liberation. We were all criminals at the time. I don't think younger people actually understand that. (The US Supreme Court's landmark decision, Lawrence v. Texas, 2003, struck down Texas' sodomy law and, by extension, invalidated sodomy laws in 13 other states, making same-sex sexual activity legal in every state, territory.) I recently did a big piece for the *Huffington Post* about why I will not serve on jury duty. And it's because I was a criminal up until about five years ago in every state. And my point was: How is this that I suddenly, without doing anything, am no longer a criminal? I didn't change.

White: When the Stonewall Riot (1969) occurred, all the gay bars were closed because New York Mayor Robert Wagner wanted to clean up the city for the 1964-65 World's Fair. Finally, they began to re-open. By that point, The Stonewall Inn was mainly a Black and Puerto Rican bar filled with drag queens. It hadn't been originally, but now it was full of kids, Black and tan kids. We felt that in closing this bar, they were trying to shut down gay bars in general. It's been forgotten that it was very hard to meet other gay people. There was no internet, no back rooms or call-in lines. Street cruising was it, and then only if you lived in a big city. So, the real story of gay people in the 50s and 60s is that they were deprived of sex. I know you're going to disagree, Felice, because you're beautiful and you had a lot of success, but I mean for average people like me, it was very hard to meet anybody. The truth is that gay liberation *was* sexual liberation. We were told in Larry Kramer's living room in 1981 by Dr. Friedman-Kien that until they knew more about the AIDS epidemic, we should just stop having sex. We all looked around at each other, the 100 or so guys there, as though he was mad.

Holleran: I came out very late in the latter half of my twenties. I was very scared of the whole thing, so I guess I'm an example of what Edmund is talking about. It was very intimidating, the whole thing. On the other hand, I just finished a memoir called *My Husband and My Wives* by Charles Beye, who grows up in Iowa City in the 30s/40s. He seemed to be blowing half the senior class.

Picano: Pre-50s, it was different.

White: That may be true, but on the other hand, look at David Leddick's book where he follows the lives of all the people who pose for photographer George Platt Lynes. He took pictures of all these cute boys who were gay at the time that he took their pictures, and eventually they all married women. Every one of them.

Picano: I hang around with a group of Santa Barbara guys in their 60s and 70s. People who were rich and have retired now. Most of them were married and had grown-up children. They didn't come out until they were in their 50s.

Holleran: The Charles Beye memoir is exactly about that. He married twice. Marries a woman two times and has four kids.

White: I think that when we were hearing the phrase "gay culture" I thought what on earth are they talking about? We're just a bunch of cocksuckers, you know. Where is this culture part? But I remember that when I first came to New York in July 1962 the second or third night I was here, I was invited to the gay restaurant, The Finale. A gay restaurant? Why would gay people want to eat with each other? By the way, I have a flash announcement to make. The other night I was sitting around with Princeton students, undergrads and grads as old as 30, but from 22 to 30, and they didn't know what the word "trick" meant.

Picano: No, it's gone. That language is gone. [See *Gay Talk: A (Sometimes Outrageous) Dictionary of Gay Slang* (aka The Queen's Vernacular), 1972, 1979, by Bruce Rodgers]

White: I explained that gay slang was essentially whore slang: to "turn a trick" …

Picano: It was all code because you didn't want people to know what you were talking about.

Holleran: With regard to Dancer from the Dance, *your words don't read like code, Bergman in* The Violet Hour *compares the criticism you endured with what Oscar Wilde encountered, namely that he was corrupting the naive young. So, I ask: Was your POV lost on readers outside of the then-idealized gay capitals of New York City and San Fransisco? Were you writing for yourself, peers?*

Holleran: I was definitely trying to get published. I hadn't written for 10 years. I had run out of any other recourse. And I had been corresponding with a friend in New York, a gay guy, who would write these very campy letters. And I thought, what if I wrote in this campy style and that started the letters and that started the book? So, I was totally in a vacuum, and I wasn't thinking of any reader. But I don't think I was aware that I had corrupted youth until David Leavitt, I think, wrote something about the fact that when he read *Dancer*, he was horrified that that's what awaited him. And I certainly didn't mean to do that.

Again, it was really written as a writer who just wants to try one more thing and I had tried everything else, and it hadn't worked.

White: It's easy to forget that this was all new material back then. Contained in the word "novel" is novelty and novelists like to write about new things. It was just too tempting to be able to write about this whole new world. In the past, fiction dealing with gay life, usually dealt with one or two people as a loving couple who were outside of the ghetto. Authors provided an ideology of how they came to be gay and the setting around them. Often their lives, the relationship ended tragically, or the person tried to reform. In contrast, our writing was different because in *Dancer from The Dance*, Andrew shows gay people living amongst other gay people, a brand-new portrayal that nobody ever had done except Genet. It was all so brand new that we, the group of us, didn't give an ideology on how characters came to be gay. We also, in Andrew's case, recognized that our themes and settings were glamorous material. Our approach was startling because gay themes were supposed to be sad and pathological. The fact that our novels were glamorous, and you might want to actually do what we wrote about if you were gay, was really unusual.

Picano: I have met so many people who said to me, "I'm gay because I read your book, *The Lure.*" They realized there was much more to gay life than being homosexual than they had ever dreamed of, because I made gay life a complex society filled with people of different ethnic and color persuasions.

Frank, I also want to address the last part of your question; you asked if my point of view was lost on the Boy Living in Fly-Over Space. When my novel *The Lure* came out, the *New York Times*, *Sunday Times*' Evan Hunter, a closeted gay author, reviewed it, essentially to eviscerate it, and that backfired. His review sold thousands of copies. The book went back to press for two more printings in the next two weeks. However, I also received death threats resulting from all that notoriety, and someone shot at me one night while I was working in my Greenwich Village office. So, the criticism was very direct.

White: Oh, God. I'd never heard that story. I would get anonymous letters that would tell me that I was going to hell or that I would be wearing a bag on my side soon, having a colostomy.

Holleran: My similar story: I was scheduled to be interviewed by a Seattle newspaper's book editor. Getting to the office was a real effort—buses, trains, flying, part of the book tour. When I got to his office he couldn't meet my eyes, casting them down on the floor saying he just couldn't go through with this because, I assumed, he was so mortified by the subject matter.

Perhaps what mortified him is what Don Shewey in his introduction to Out Front: Contemporary Gay & Lesbian Plays, *means by shallow hedonism, empty narcissism, or non-judgmentally expressed, that rarefied freedom, intense communication, energy and creativity that you're all talking about, that gay people were finally reading novels about gay people in gay life with other gay people. The post-Stonewall era when sex was above ground and enjoyed in abandoned city piers, parks, on rooftops, the trucks.*

Picano: I long for the days of shallow hedonism, empty narcissism. I'm so glad I was young during all of that. I really am. I think young people would appreciate it today.

White: I don't know what Shewey is talking about. Is he saying that before Stonewall, people were empty narcissists and hedonists but not afterward? I mean the big change after Stonewall was "clonism." In other words, before gay liberation, the idea was the "boy" in you. When you turned 30 in the 50s, which I can remember, other gay people would stage a funeral for you because your life was over at 30. As an older man you might by some luck get a cute boy in his white jeans and powder blue cashmere sweater. Then they would grow up and turn 30 and their life was over. But I think suddenly what happened in the 70s, partly resulting from gay liberation, was that now you had two mustachioed 35-year-olds falling in love with each other. They could be equals, could both be lawyers and they could take turns fucking each other. It was all new.

Holleran: Do you think that represented North America because I remember at the time realizing that in Latin cultures, certainly South America, they couldn't understand how two men could be equal.

White: It was absolutely American and maybe Northern Europe, kind of a Protestant thing. I don't think so in the

Catholic world or certainly not in the "garlic belt" as we called it, France, Italy and Spain.

Picano: I think it was American and then it transferred. I refer to it as the generation of 1975, because I had been going out to Fire Island sporadically from the late 60s, staying with older people, but all of a sudden, an entire new group of 30-35-year-old hot guys with mustaches appeared in the summer of 1975. Like a whole new generation. Minor muscles, it wasn't big muscles then. That's I think what changed everything.

Is it a given that one had to have participated back then, at least in a minimum way, in order to talk about it with any creativity or credibility?
Picano: Well, there were so few gay people out at that time, or even halfway out, that you pretty much knew most of the gay people in Manhattan. It wasn't that difficult if you got around. If you went to clubs, if you went to resorts, if you went to parties, you ended up meeting most of the people you wanted to meet. It was a small number of people.

White: The downtown scene was very small. Like Fran Lebowitz said, everyone who read Andy Warhol's *Interview* knew each other.

Holleran: But there was resentment against that too. I remember when our books came out people would ask "Why do you always have to write about 'fast lane gays?'" Why was it always about Manhattan and the urban scene? Leaving the impression that there were vast members of gays in small towns and other places who weren't having their lives written about. And I suppose that was true to a degree.

White: But they were all in the closet. Andrew, I was criticized for this when writing *States of Desire* (1980), for not covering a lot of minority groups and rural gays. The main reason was that unless you lived there and cultivated those people over several years, you couldn't meet them.

In contrast to the "rural" dilemma of meeting other gays, Susan Sontag summarized post Stonewall as a time when "many male homosexuals reconstituted themselves as something like an ethnic group, one whose distinctive folkloric custom was sexual voracity, and the institutions of urban homosexual life became a sexual delivery system of unprecedented speed, efficiency and volume." And just when we thought it couldn't get any faster, came the internet and now Grindr. Visibility is high but has the sexual delivery system changed?

Picano: I don't know, I think that there's a lot more hookups from what I've experienced but the sex is lousier than it ever was. And I mean, really, really terrible. Everybody should read any version of *The Joy of Gay Sex* to give them tips. (White and Picano each completed a version with psychiatrist Dr. Charles Silverstein with whom White had to end his therapeutic relationship before beginning the collaboration.)

What's making the sex lousy?

Picano: During the 70s the worst thing you could say about somebody is: Oh, he may be beautiful, have lots of money, be famous, but he's bad at sex. That was a killer. Nowadays, people seem unable to do really basic things well in bed.

Holleran: When I first heard that people were going to Tea Dance in the Fire Island Pines and standing there looking at Grindr on their smartphones, I thought this is a scream. What does that mean you go to Tea Dance and you're on Grindr?

Picano: It had already reached a point that the last time I went to the Eagles Nest it was called S&M, as in stand and model, because nobody was hooking up.

White: I think this is a general phenomenon. I just reviewed A.M. Holmes new novel *May We Be Forgiven* for *The New York Review of Books*. I quoted a passage in which she says: Everybody talks about how important family is, but when they finally get together all they do is sit at the table and look at their telephones. Trying to communicate with other people is difficult because virtual reality is more acceptable than real reality. Face to face, nobody can really tolerate the ups and downs of family life or real intimacy. It's much more promising to have virtual relationships.

Holleran: I agree, except for one thing. I have to ask, Is this because of our age? Should we ask a 26-year-old? I suspect for them, not having known anything else, that they view these interactions as much the human comedy as we experienced them without the computer, but I don't know.

Picano: I did an editorial for *The Huffington Post* called *Children of the Hive* and during this time my car was in the shop and I was using buses. I was observing people on the phone and how they related. Older people usually conferred messages back and forth, sometimes very briefly. But children and young people and teenagers would talk for 30 minutes on a bus without saying anything of importance. I assumed they were stroking each other the way bees do in hives, that we are forming a new kind of hive mentality, establishing that being in communication in some way is more important than actually communicating anything.

White: Back to Sontag, Frank. If you're referring to an essay she wrote called *Fascinating Fascism*, it's a very foolish and hostile essay in which she equates American leather queens with fascists, a very primitive attitude and very arrogant and stupid, I think. She has great insights on millions of topics, this was not one of them. Studies have shown that S&M people are often vegetarian, more sensitive to the sight of pain than ordinary people are, against capital punishment. To call them fascists is just ignorant. And Jean Genet, who was attracted to real Nazis in their uniforms, said that he was a Communist and he was very clear his politics had nothing to do with his sexual taste. This kind of reductionism that people have, and I think Sontag is guilty of it, is extremely narrow-minded and foolish.

Felice, in Bergman's preface to **The Violet Hour** *he writes that* *you informed him at great length about what you see as the errors of his ways. What were Bergman's errors?*

Picano: Like most academics, he likes neat little theories. And unlike most of them, he could not be persuaded that he was wrong. Bergman divides the *VQ* into two groups; those who circulated around Holleran and those who circulated around Edmund White. And then he places me as the outsider. Guys, was I ever the outsider?

White: Well, no, you had your own fans and...

Picano: Right, I introduced the two of you (White and Holleran). Do you remember? Because you didn't know each other until I introduced you at Stu Roder's place at Fire Island Pines. Barry Walker made us all dinner. While he and I cleaned up, you talked. Do you remember that? That was the first time you guys met. And it took me about two months to get you together.

Holleran: Yeah, that's true, you introduced us, but I don't remember any of that...

White: I don't either, but I'm senile. I don't remember...

Picano: Here's the other thing regarding Bergman. I was dating George Whitmore when The Violet Quill began and throughout its existence. After Chris Cox and Edmund broke up, I remained close to Cox. And I was seeing him almost daily in the weeks before he died. Also, I was very close to Robert

(Ferro) and Michael (Grumley) long after the group ended. And I spoke to Robert maybe a few hours before he died. So, I don't think I was outside of anything.

White: No, no, of course not. And I was close to Chris Cox and we had been boyfriends. And then I had a sexual affair with George Whitmore.

Picano: The other thing he writes about, and he assures readers that Edmund White was always the best known of us at the time we got together. Edmund deserved to be better known, but he wasn't better known until later. Holleran had garnered enormous publicity through *Dancer* in 1978, before we started meeting. And as for being connected up in literary circles, Allen Ginsberg had asked me to join him in a poetry reading at Hunter College way back in 1974. My first book was a PEN Hemingway Finalist in 1975. I had a *New York Times* paperback bestseller in 1977, all before we began meeting. Bergman just didn't do his homework.

The Gay Writers Who Changed America

Felice, Andrew, Edmund: Christopher Bram's **Eminent Outlaws: The Gay Writers Who Changed America,** *opens a chapter by citing your dairies as an "entertaining account" of the Violet Quill period. He writes "It is sometimes claimed that the Violet Quill as a group created the new gay literature.... Holleran later wrote a fine essay about Robert Ferro after Ferro's death, where he downplayed the Violet Quill...called*

*it a 'dessert and short story' club. White in his memoirs and
autobiographical fiction never mentions the group at all." Does
he have it right?*

Picano: First of all, let's consider the source. This is somebody
who admittedly can no longer sell a novel to a publisher, right?
And who thought he was doing the great bright thing back in
the 80s when he sold one of his books to the movies. And now,
essentially, he doesn't seem to have a career. So, I think we have
to be very careful about who Christopher Bram is as an author
nowadays. Also, he never interviewed any of us that I'm aware
of. Did he interview you guys?

Holleran: No.

Picano: Which he should have done. If you're writing about
living people, wouldn't you at least call them up. The other
thing is it's to none of our advantages to admit that we've been a
group. If we want to be strictly ruthless and ambitious, yeah, we
belonged to this little group a long time ago, but it doesn't mean
anything in the great arc of our magnificent careers. I mean, let's
be honest.

White: My memoirs do not cover that period. I've written three
memoirs, one of which is still unpublished, about my Paris
years. I never wrote about that period, so that's why I didn't
mention it. In *City Boy*, I write about the early 60s and the early
70s and I don't mention the Violet Quill. I could write an essay
about it, although we only met eight times.

Picano: I did a piece about Robert Ferro that was in *Loss within Loss*, an anthology that you (Edmund) put together. That was one of the few times I've written about the group.

Holleran: Well, I think two things are true. I think it was a short story and dessert club and we did only meet eight times, if that. And it was pleasant and I don't think we put any huge store into it, except it was an agreeable thing to do at the time. But I also think that we've got an incredible amount of mileage out of this. I understand that no artist wants to be grouped, an artist wants to be unique, but on the other hand, we've had a wonderful series of panels, and meetings, and things.

Picano: Nobody else that we knew, like Richard Howard or Jimmy Merrill, nobody, would discuss gay literature. They said gay literature is all porn. Isn't that what they told you, Edmund? That's what they told me. What do you want to write something gay for? Do something literary.

White: Yes, that's right. I remember.

Holleran: Edmund, who's the figure in *City Boy* that does that to you?

White: Richard Poirier. He blew up at me at a party. (Then-*Raritan* editor Richard Poirier became "furious" with White for suggesting that there may be "gay" fiction, poetry, even a gay sensibility.)

Holleran: So, Poirier tells you that you're a fool for wanting to write about gay life, for wanting to be considered a gay writer...

White: His position is actually a lot more divisible than that, but he started screaming at me for talking about a gay sensibility or gay literature. He felt that literature had to be universalist. And so does every person in France think it has to be universal. There is no gay fiction in France. There is no Black fiction. There's no Jewish fiction. It's all universal. Everyone insists on that. And no French person has ever said Yes to the question, Are you a gay writer? Not one. I now can see what Poirier's (saying), but I felt that he was very intolerant of what was essentially a chance to explore new material in fiction. Back then at that party, I was the unpublished or just published writer and always the youngest person in these circles. So, I was unusually sensitive to these disputes, but nobody else was. We were very friendly before he died. I saw him two or three times at parties and he was extremely friendly.

Holleran: Well, Edmund, you weren't a completely unknown transitional figure between generations and cultural things.

White: You're right. I was a friend of Richard Howard, Poirier, David Kalstone, James Merrill, Susan Sontag. They were all considerably older.

Holleran: They were part of a generation that regarded anything explicitly gay as essentially provincial and second rate. Then you went ahead pursuing the role they had occupied, but you used gay material throughout. In a way, you insisted on something.

White: We should be fair because Richard Howard very early on wrote gay poems and James Merrill in his profession turned to it. Ashbery never did. Sontag never did.

Holleran: Let me clarify. I'm not judging these people in any way. To look back at another generation or another time and feel superior to it, I think is one of the most stupid things that people do.

Picano: You know, Edmund, I always pointed out to people who say that gay literature is not universal that the first accepted piece of literature in Western culture which is the Gilgamesh epic, which has a very large gay or homosexual component to it. It's half of that book.

Felice, as drawn from your incredible memory and personal journals, Art and Sex in Greenwich Village *outlines the history of Sea Horse Press and the combined work of Sea Horse and three other presses, known as Gay Presses of New York. Today, there's Chelsea Station Editions, Magnus Books. Harrington Press is gone. Not to compare, but who's out there today bringing out new names that you're looking at, aware of?*
Picano: I'm pulling for Chelsea Station. I think the most extraordinary LGBT press around today is run by a lesbian who writes under the name of Radclyffe. It's called Bold Strokes Books. They've opened up a gay male division called Liberty Press. Last year, they put out 78 new books.

Holleran: Mainstream publishers, you have to notice, are bringing out an awful lot of gay books. Even so, it's a balkanized world out there for gay manuscripts.

White: Well Jonathan Galassi came out and he's bringing out a lot of gay books. Michael Lowenthal's new novel, *The Paternity Test*, came out from the University of Wisconsin.

Picano: Raphael Kadushin is doing wonderful books over there.

Which writers, gay, straight, excite you today?
White: I like A.M. Holmes…she's written a lot about gay subject matter. Many of her characters from her first book on have been gay. She'll write a novel about a straight boy who has a gay father who comes out, asking how the son deals with his father. I like Sarah Schulman's writing a great deal. Watch for James Salter's new book *All That Is* that I've just read in galleys. He also wrote *A Sport and a Pastime*.

Picano: The Hispanic American queer men and women writers of today are the most unique. They have the most to bitch about and the most to change in their lives. I co-edited an anthology last year, Ambientes: New Queer Latino Writing (co-edited with Lazaro Lima), because I think there's so much really great writing out there, I've also been reading some Canadian poets, S. McDonald wrote the only interesting transvestite piece of literature I've come across; a group of very good poems called *Confessions of an Empty Purse*. And David Bateman wrote a wonderful book called *'tis pity*. I find them very accomplished and new. I like the idea of women writing as men as Dale Chase does quite fearlessly in her books. And for the long run at the moment, I like both Trebor Healy and Kevin Killian the most.

Edmund, you mentioned Schulman. In her **Gentrification of the Mind,** *she reprints portions of interviews she did with you and Andrew Sullivan as a way of illustrating your fear, shared by many, including myself, of being marginalized by younger people, especially but not exclusively around AIDS. You say, "It's one thing to think that we all went through this together and survived and here's my story of what I went through. It's going to be another thing to have nobody want to read those stories."*

White: Well, I'm always reminded of a book by Vera Britten called, *The Testament of Youth.* She was a nurse in World War I and then went to Oxford. She was only maybe two years older than the other students, but they would all roll their eyes and start laughing whenever she had mentioned the war. That was all old news, and they didn't want to think about it. I think it's the same thing with AIDS. The whole AIDS period has been forgotten the way the Banana War is forgotten in *One Hundred Years of Solitude* by Colombian author Gabriel García Márquez that tells the multi-generational story of the Buendía family. Nobody wants to talk about it; the fact that hundreds of people were killed, forget it. Although the other day when I talked to Sarah Schulman at a reading she gave, she said young people are quite interested in the history of AIDS. I don't know if they're so much interested in the *literature* of AIDS, but they're responding quite a bit to the new documentary films, *United in Anger,* she co-produced with Jim Hubbard. There's also *How* to *Survive a Plague* about ACT UP and the Treatment Action Group.

Holleran: I loved *Plague,* saw it twice and afterwards wrote an email to Larry Kramer saying that I had just seen it and that I liked it very much. He wrote something back that was very funny and shocking, insights you don't get in the movie. Here's what ties what you just said about young people not wanting to read AIDS literature: I think *only* the literature is going to be able to tell the full story of the plague. There were so many scenes in that movie where you're wondering, you know, what's going on and who is the good person and who is the bad person?

Picano: I'll give an example of that. The Vito Russo movie in which I have a very brief moment, is out. Russo is turned into an All-American hero because that's the only way that young people can see people of our generation, as heroes or losers, and it's complete bullshit. I love Vito. He was a great person, but he's not a great American hero. Or if he is, 10,000 of us, 20,000 of us were heroes. I'm afraid it's all being distorted. And poor Vito might well be spinning in his grave to Bambi, shown as a figure addressing people from balconies when he was such a modest guy. The movie is so unlike him and yet that's what the movie does. (Russo came to one meeting of the group and read portions of his celebrated *The Celluloid Closet.*)

What meaning do each of you find in the AIDS experience, looking back at the roles each of you played, the roles that people think you played, the roles that may look different now?

Picano: In the early 90s, I addressed the Gay Journalist Association which had been spending an entire weekend congratulating itself on how far they had gotten. They had gotten some NBC anchor to appear. I said to people, as I was soundly booed to the point where I left the building: You know, in the future, AIDS which dominates our lives is going to be seen as a tiny little blip in gay history and gay culture. Everybody will wonder why we spent so much time dealing with it, I think in the future no one's going to pay attention to it. They just howled, threw notebooks at me and it turned out, I was right.

White: I think that will be true, Felice. It's like the history of Syphilis or Tuberculosis in the 19th century, everybody had it and some wrote about it, including Alphonse Daudet who wrote a translated book called *In the Land of Pain*. What did AIDS do for us? I think it gave us a good subject. Yeats said there are two great subjects for any writer – love and death; and AIDS had both. I wrote a novel, *The Married Man*, which I think shows some of that, although Larry Kramer criticized it by saying it wasn't even a love story. So, I think AIDS was a subject that people were tempted to cover. Andrew, I remember you saying you wanted to write what became *Ground Zero: Chronicle of a Plague* (later reissued as *Ground Zero: Chronicle of a Plague, Revisited*).

Holleran: I'm listening to you both thinking that I don't know how to express this. When I watched *How to Survive a Plague*, I didn't know what I felt about ACT UP and the times during those events. One of the good things about the documentary is that it's filmed as it is happening, so there's no editorializing. You really get to decide what you feel about it because you're basically watching movies that were made at the time those meetings and demonstrations were held. And part of me agrees that AIDS is going to be a blip, but at the time I thought to myself, this has nothing to do with anything except a virus. This is simply a medical thing. But by the time I finished watching *Plague*, I thought to myself, for better or worse, that the movement was in a way, the gay civil rights movement at its climax. After AIDS and ACT UP, two things happened: gay life was completely out of the closet as a byproduct of talking about AIDS. The straight community had to become aware of things that they had never heard of before. AIDS brought gay life completely out of the closet. The other thing was the straight community gained respect for gay people so, as a result, they did not just die. Their death had meaning beyond their years.

Picano: AIDS certainly changed the younger generation and their whole attitude toward everything. But I'm trying to remember, do you remember, Edmund, when we were at those meetings at Paul Popham's apartment. (Popham was the first president of the Gay Men's Health Crisis, 1981-85. He was the basis for the Bruce Niles character in Larry Kramer's *The Normal Heart*, one of the first plays to address AIDS.) We figured out the group we were forming had to be called Health Crisis, very specifically, so it would not have any political import but only be medical.

White: I remember the reasoning behind the name, Gay

Men's Health Crisis, was that first of all we had had so many unpleasant experiences with lesbians that we wanted to say, well this is something happening to gay men. And not have to do the whole LGBT thing. Now, mind you, later, lesbians like Sarah Schulman became active in the movement, which actually healed the rift between lesbians and gay men. But as I recall, calling AIDS a health crisis was a way to suggest that it was serious but would not last forever. (CDC, 2009: g/bi men are 2% of the U.S. population but accounted for 61% of all new HIV infections. The number of gay men infected may be as high as 1 in 8 with 1/5 not aware of their infection. 30,000 gay men, mostly young men of color, are newly diagnosed each year.)

Writing Gay Characters

Don Shewey in Out Front *writes: "Perhaps the essential strangeness of being gay is being something other than what one was brought up to be." Kids today are out at young ages and raised openly. If you had a character(s) in a current piece, how would you portray them? Through what nuanced voice?*

White: I don't agree with Shewey at all because I just had an 18-year-old student who wrote a very tortured piece about being Catholic and coming out in the confessional booth and being sent to a psychologist who was supposed to do reparative therapy. Young people are part of their parents' generation much more than we realize. If you want to know what young people think, ask a 30-year-old, not an 18-year-old, because an 18-year-old is engulfed in his parents' value system. And if he's a Mormon or Catholic, I mean, we're the most religious country in the Western world but thankfully the US is growing less religious; nonetheless, the three Monotheistic religions with their horrible approach to homosexuality still prevail in America.

Picano: I always wrote as though people were assumed to be gay. From early in my writing my gay characters were people who were out and comfortable with it as much as possible. I was always assuming that would be true. On the other hand, I've been aware of the fact that many children continue to go through problems with their parents. The madness isn't over. Kids were out when we were young and were being harassed then. I came to believe that some of the West Village homeless and alcoholic characters that we knew in the 60s and 70s like Marsha P. Johnson and Bambi were outcasts originally because they couldn't hide their queerness from the family. Every generation has to deal with it in its own way.

It doesn't quite match up. People say, well, no one under 30 really cares. And I keep saying, somebody's doing all this bullying.
Picano: Exactly, exactly.

Holleran: It's a brave new world and it's not.

Picano: Even so, I try to write about gay life as though everybody's accepting it or that it's the way to be because in some ways, when you're writing fiction, you're writing idealized life, no matter what you try to do.

White: That's what poet James Meredith called "moral sculpture," when you pretend that things are much more advanced than they are. That people are much more liberated than they are. I remember when I worked on *The Joy of Gay Sex* with Charles Silverstein, I created a kind of persona for myself who was much more comfortable with being gay than I actually was. (Charles Silverstein has written a memoir, *For the Ferryman*, published by Chelsea Station Editions.)

Picano: I had an interesting experience with Charles, who was one of the people behind the American Psychiatric Association removing homosexuality from its list of illnesses. We worked on two subsequent versions of *The Joy of Gay Sex*. I found that he was less comfortable with his gayness than I was. He actually developed more tolerance as we went along and got older.

White: Well, he was very inexperienced. He came out late and he went right into a relationship.

Edmund, you wrote in the foreword of The Faber Book of Short Fiction *that since no one is brought up and recognized as being gay, the moment he recognizes the difference, he must account for it. "Such accounts are kind of primitive gay fiction." Is that idea still alive?*
White: I think so. Very few gay people are brought up to be gay. Oh, maybe some male prostitutes in India are brought up to be gay, but I mean regular people are not brought up to be gay. So, discovering that is a huge change in your life, when you have to come out, if you're 13 or 30, you have to acknowledge that this

is a new set of rules for you.

I remember asking Silverstein once, what is the single biggest problem that married men who come out have to deal with? And he said, loss of status. I just read figures yesterday that said that gay people are poorer than straight people.

Holleran: And always have been.

White: People used to talk about how we had all this disposable income, maybe that was true. But we have less income than regular people.

Right, but that was at a time when everyone thought every homosexual was a white privileged, well-educated man, an image peddled by gay media run by white privileged, well-educated men.
White: Yes, that's right.

Manly Men

We're all older now, of course, and Andrew, you wrote in the foreword to The Man I Might Become, *edited by Bruce Shenitz, on the theme of becoming men. Felice, you had a piece in that volume too.*
Holleran: Horror, horror. When I saw that in your email with the questions you were going to ask, Frank, and I thought that is such a huge question, a chill came over me. Because it's the kind of thing you do at the end of your life, which is to express

yourself. It's just an enormous question. And I don't know the answer. Part of me is pleased that I did become who, I guess, I thought I wanted to be. Part of reaching this stage in life, I think, is going through to the opposite side of your feelings, feeling things you didn't originally. Well, I can't even go on. It's too good a question. That's a question I'm going to have to write about rather than to answer verbally. Somebody take this away.

Picano: Frank, to seriously answer your question, at the age of 16 or 17, I pretty much destroyed my entire idea of what other people expected of me. I was really part of a counterculture. And as opposed to Edmund and Andrew, I came out very easily because it was part of my way of destroying the entire picture people had of my life. I was going to be new and different in every way. I was going to be radical. I was going to be politicked. I was going to live in a commune. People used to shout, "Cut your hair! Take that earring off!" And that's the way I've remained. Poet Edward Field (Lambda Award Winner, 1992, *Counting Myself Lucky, Selected Poems 1963-1992*) is trying to sell a profile he did with me to *The New Yorker* called *The Last Hippie*. He might be right. That might be who I am. And I still feel like the person I aimed to be, once I got rid of all of my parents' conceptions or misconceptions.

Holleran: What is your answer, Edmund?

White: I'm with you, I would have to write an essay about it. I think writers are bad at discussing general questions or philosophical questions. And if they can discuss them, they have to meditate on them. It's a good subject whenever somebody's of two minds about something. Am I the man I wanted to be? I don't like a totalizing of life. I think that life is just this moment, and then the next moment, and the next. Totalizing one's life is a kind of post-Christian thing, to summarize your life. Summarizing your life is like a substitute for heaven or hell, a way of placing a grade next to your name.

Summarizing is a state of judgment?
White: Yes, which I don't like because we've known so many people who have died of AIDS or even of Alzheimer's and so on, and they become totally reduced to that right before they die. Are we supposed to say that is the way they really were? Is that supposed to reveal some truth about their lives? And I don't mean to go on about that, I'm ducking the question because I just think the question has to be questioned.

Writing Now

A reader once commented to poet Marianne Moore: "Your poems are difficult to read." She replied, paraphrased: They're difficult to write. At any age writing is a physically draining exercise. How does the process feel to you now?
Picano: Well writing for me, if it's for two hours, is a lot less draining than having sex for two hours. And I don't have sex for two hours.

But it wasn't always that way?
Picano: It wasn't. I think I've written my best two novels recently

and joyfully, and I continue to do so. I don't find it painful in any way. Writing is wonderful when I do it, not draining. I have had very draining, emotionally draining circumstances when writing books. When I was writing *Like People in History*, which was all about friends and lovers, I would have to stop because I found myself weeping as I was keyboarding. But that doesn't happen anymore. I've gone beyond that. What about you guys?

Holleran: I still take pleasure in writing. But the part that is difficult now and what happens to all writers, mentioned by Bram in *Eminent Outlaws*, is the problem of the mindless writer sitting before the computer and what's happened to publishing. In the past, we were all in a rather comfortable relationship with the outer world in the sense that we thought that if we wrote anything interesting or wrote it well, that it could be printed and received at the other end. Now there's this feeling of diving into an empty swimming pool. Writers can no longer be sure. I don't think publishers know either. I don't know what's out there anymore, how people are reading (iPads, Nooks, traditional books), what they're reading, and what the act of reading is like anymore. Sometimes I think I'm just like a woman making lace, sitting here in my little room spinning things because I get pleasure from it and I'm not going to stop just because I don't know how to market my lace.

White: I agree. We may be the last generation of people who believed in the myth of the writer. And who have so far have been able to get published, but it's constantly threatened. Last year literary fiction was down 20%. On the other hand, a friend of mine whose book went out of print was taken up by Amazon and he's made more money than he's made in his whole life from Amazon, which gives authors 70%.

Picano: All of my early paperbacks are going on Kindle.

Holleran: This brings us back to David Bergman. We were talking about just this in a recent email in which he said to me, and I'm paraphrasing, that the age of reading lasted no longer than the age of human sacrifice. That years from now people are going to look back at this strange epoch when people sat in front of things and looked at symbols on the page. In one's despair, one thinks like that.

White: I feel very strange teaching creative writing to 18-year-olds and I'm so grateful to know that most of my students are studying biochemistry or physics, that they only take creative writing as a one off, that they can't major in it.

Picano: I won't teach writing. I teach literature. I'll teach reading, but not writing. I think communication and reading is changing, but not that much. I was just at the West Hollywood Book Fair and it was bigger than ever. The question has the expanded world of communication, publishing become too big? That literally was one of the topics because there are so many readers. There are so many writers. There are so many people interested.

White: Aren't there more writers than readers now? Here's a

change...there used to be 10 or 20 books a year that everyone had to read. That's gone completely. Our whole culture has been diversified. There are now 300 TV channels. It used to be that you would stand by the water cooler and discuss last night's episode of some shared show. Now there's no such thing. There's no focus for a dialogue in our culture anymore.

Picano: Reminds me of a David Bowie film in which he plays a spaceman, *The Man Who Fell to Earth*. You see him looking at 25 television sets on all at once. That's what the future is going to look like. Our attention will be like that.

White: I think people's brains are being rewired to only have an attention span of three seconds or something.

Holleran: That's too long. And it seems to me the presumption is if you can type, that means you can write.

Picano: The changes have also given good writers a chance to get out there, writers who were closed out of the system beforehand.

White: Lots of people, especially in genre fiction, will write a book and just directly post it online where it gets lots of hits. Then he'll write a sequel to that. After about three rounds, he has a fan base. The idea seems to work better in genre fiction than in so-called literary fiction.

Remembrance Past

Paul Auster in a memoir anecdote writes: A woman approaches James Joyce at a party asking to shake the hand that wrote Ulysses. *Joyce is said to have replied: "Let me remind, madam, that this hand has done many other things as well." What other things have each of you done as well? Hope to do in the future?*

Picano: I garden, I cook. In my "Last Will and Testament," I specifically wrote that no section of my journals or other personal writings can be published after my death that eliminates all of my recreational drug use and my many sexual advances. It has to all be there or it cannot be used. That's also specified in the arrangement that I did with the Beinecke Library at Yale University, regarding publication of my papers. I just don't want my life taken out of context. They can publish it if they include a representational sample. Which includes, you know, I took two Tuinal, then blew a priest. And then wrote my masterpiece.

White: I used to have a French boyfriend who said that if I wasn't a writer, I could open a restaurant because I am still a fairly good cook.

Holleran: I can't think of anything, really, that I'd want readers to know. It's charming to think that people would want to know because as we've just been discussing, this whole glamorous idea of the writer is so much a thing of the past now.

Speaking of once-glamorous writers, Edmund, in The Farewell Symphony, *you write "history is nothing but feuds and fashionable complications." What delicious feuds are you all enjoying today, about any topic, gay literature, anything?*

White: I seem to get attacked more than anybody else in reviews. For example, Daniel Mendelsohn, who writes for *The New York Review of Books*. It's not an active feud, but I wouldn't cross the room to talk to him at a party. You know, every single nasty review I've ever had is from a gay man. I have never been badly reviewed by a woman or a straight man.

Queer Theory

Edmund, you reviewed David Halperin's new book How to Be Gay *in* The New York Review of Books. *Given all the changes since Stonewall and The Violet Quill era, how is one to be gay?*
Picano: I've read the review of Halperin's book and want to say something about Queer Theory. At base I think it's utterly homophobic. And not one of the academics involved in Queer Theory can see it. When they finally wake up, I think a lot of people are going to be really embarrassed. Queer Theory is homophobic in that it denies essentially that there is homosexuality. It just denies it, period. The theory says homosexuality is a performative act. Well, making a baby is a performative act too. All we do in life are performative acts. So, I don't see how homosexuality is meaningless compared to anything else in life. I think it's just really deep bullshit.

*There's another review of Halperin's book (*Times Literary Supplement, *Oct. 17, 2012) by Richard Davenport-Hines, a British scholar. He wrote: "The tragedy of queer studies is that a subject of exceptional importance to humanity is left in the* *clutches of show-offs who reduce it to self-centered banality."*

Picano: Written off. Even the founder of the school, Eve Sedgwick, before she died, said we've made a mistake. That's my take. Douglas Sadownick, Antioch University, has written a paper about Queer Theory on which I've been consulted. He's taking the whole school to task on it in a very point-by-point manner.

Working on It

Are any of you working on something you'd like our readers to keep in mind?

Picano: I just finished a historic novel set in pre-Homeric Greece called *Notes from a Golden Age* which rewrites literature from the beginning.

Holleran: Well, I'm working on a lot of stuff that I want to get out of the computer and I'm having trouble getting out of the computer. Right now, I'm really publishing just articles and essays in *The Gay and Lesbian Review*. I think that's about it for now.

Picano: I do want to talk about one thing. The fact that you're talking to us many years after our most famous gay books came out, I think says something. And I appreciate your attention and I'm sure so do Andrew and Edmund. This interview speaks to something that I found interesting. Living in Los Angeles, which I've been doing now for about 19 years, just you get a different concept of what life is like. For a period of about four, five years, every time somebody would ask me to do something as an author I would do it. They would say, you know, Felice, you're a star. That compliment stopped having any kind of meaning for me and I wondered about it. Around the same time, I had become an escort to a group of elderly Hollywood actresses who used to call themselves The Brassy Old Dames. They didn't hire us, they just used us socially because they needed some presentable guys who could wear tuxedos to take them out to the Oscars and to other parties around Los Angeles, like award ceremonies which is still a big bullshit thing here. So, the very old and still beautiful Loretta Young became one of my dates about two years before she died. She was tiny, but very pretty.

I explained to her that everybody says to me, Oh, you're a star! And she said to me, Felice, you have to understand, one is a star not only because you shine brightly, but because you shine brightly for a long, long time. As she had done. That's my final statement.

THE MARTIN DUBERMAN READER: THE ESSENTIAL HISTORICAL, BIOGRAPHIC AND AUTOBIOGRAPHICAL WRITINGS

Martin Duberman (born 1930) has the style of a public intellectual of a bygone era. His interview and review of *The Martin Duberman Reader: The Essential Historical, Biographic and Autobiographical Writings* is an overview of gay lives and times, including the Black, anti-Vietnam War, and Women's movements, providing benchmark understandings of what has come before us, by a public figure comparable to Gore Vidal, Mary McCarthy, and Norman Podhoretz.

Duberman is a warm guy unimpressed with himself in a refreshing way. He made us iced coffee from an earlier brewed pot. Relaxed, he allowed time for us to gel before starting our interview. He was attentive to my comfort in setting up a small electronic recording device. An unnamed man came and went quietly through his living room as we talked. I respect boundaries and didn't inquire. As we discussed his work, opinions, and deeply held beliefs, he was quick in a non-defensive way to point out his own inconsistencies, but not at his own expense. He simply acknowledges that what we know and hold true today may change by tomorrow.

I was pleased to learn that he found my second Edmund

White interview "very impressive. It all reads so well....". We convened on June 15, the day after *The Nation* magazine, where Duberman is a regular contributor, held a memorial service for Donald Shaffer, a longtime financial supporter of the abolitionist publication founded in 1865. I attended with Shaffer's grandson Alan Kennedy Shaffer.

The day before we talked, Duberman email that he'd skimmed my questions noting "they seem unusually shrewd." Afterword, he emailed to tell me that "I think the interview does represent my views – which is much more unusual than you might think!"

〜 ᵐ〉

Your latest book is The Martin Duberman Reader: The Essential Historical, Biographic and Autobiographical Writings. *Since you are so prolific, how did you select the table of contents?*

Well, when the title says "essential," you're never sure if a given volume accurately represents one's work. Selection is very tricky because you don't know what your readers know. For example, if you start talking about Paul Robeson does the average reader, whoever that is, have enough background so that you can get straight into Robeson and Communism or must you cover all the background as well? Selection can be difficult especially in this country because so few Americans know any history; many approach a book without having any built-in context. Basically, I chose sections that pleased me and which I thought best represented the book at hand. That was my process.

Regarding history, a Reader essay delineates a genealogy of gay and lesbian politics during the 1960s and after. You helped found the National Gay Task Force, later renamed the National Gay and Lesbian Task Force to recognize the role of women. Let's go through some organizations and issues and try to assess their politics at the time, left, center, right or something else.

My answers will reflect how I currently perceive those organizations, though at the time they formed I may have perceived them differently.

What about The Gay Liberation Front (GLF)?

It was formed just after Stonewall, 1970 probably, a direct result of the riots themselves. It was the birth essentially of a new movement. GLF was in contrast to the homophile movement, as it was called then, which preceded and is represented by the Mattachine Society and Daughters of Bilitis.

Next came the Gay Activist Alliance. Did that group have dotted lines back to the gay men and women in the 1960s anti-Vietnam war movement? Did they apply what they learned to their political circumstances?

I think without the 1960s having happened there probably would not have been the Stonewall Riots at the end of the decade. And by that, I mean we were all being enormously influenced by developments during the 1960s. Without being fully conscious of it, or in some cases only partially conscious.

I regard the Black Movement as the granddaddy of all the movements that followed thereafter. What Blacks were saying then about themselves also applied directly to gay people. Blacks were saying, "Yeah, we may be different but that doesn't make us inferior. In fact, in some ways our differences may make us superior to mainstream white values." Thus, the slogan "Black is beautiful." And even though at the time I was still in therapy trying to get cured, trying to turn heterosexual, I heard that sentiment. During the 1960s all this was repeated over and over again. So eventually, even if your ears were closed, the message did get through that it's okay to be different.

Does the experience of being different – gay, Black or both – suggest a level of superiority or insight because the ignominy of oppression makes one stronger?

I would say if oppression doesn't kill you, there's the chance it will make you stronger. The gay movement also learned from earlier outsiders like women in the 1960s. The Women's Movement began before Stonewall and we got those messages, too, about gender nonconformity, about androgyny being the ideal model rather than dividing up human characteristics between one gender and another. They held that everyone should aim at incorporating all those characteristics within oneself, whether or not one's genitalia was male or female. Overall, the 1960s was an enormously creative and challenging period. The period made everybody who was at least partially available to listen rethink who we long thought we were.

In a Reader essay, you write about the 1950s, when youth were criticized as inert, and the 1960s, when they were portrayed as too passionate. "Youth culture," created by Hollywood back then, was a huge cash cow. Many people rushed to see James Dean and Elvis movies. Is that Friedrich Hegel's dialectic at work? A thesis, antithesis, and eventual synthesis or rejection? Does one decade nurse the seeds of the next?

These rigid divisions between decades don't make any sense because along with James Dean there was, of course, the Beats, Allen Ginsberg, Kerouac. There were also the Beatles. They were all subversive elements but the overall tone, I think, of the 1950s was the tone set by Senator Joseph McCarthy. People were afraid of being "exposed" as deviant in regard to mainstream values. So, you did your best – remember too that most people did their best in the 1950s to conceal aspects of themselves that they thought were unacceptable to the mainstream.

Demarcations of decades are not rigid or arbitrary. You often read that the 1960s began with the assassination of JFK in 1963 and that's when the 1970s actually began. Demarcations are fluid…

Regarding demarcations, surveys and anecdotes indicate many men like to have sex with other men yet do not identify as "gay." I've heard guys say "no rainbows, no parades" but that they still want to have sex with a guy. They often have a wife and kids or a girlfriend. Without trying to be politically correct, how do we explain this phenomenon?

Well, this is especially true in minority communities. Many Black and Hispanic men will not adopt the label *gay* because it's white identified. From its inception, the organized political movement has been dominated by whites. Black and Hispanics have sometimes formed their own groups, but they have remained small in comparison with, say, the National Gay Task Force or the Human Rights Campaign.

So, it's a refusal of an identity that doesn't resemble their life experience rather than a disagreement about behavior; it's all the same behavior but their cultural encoding of it is different?
Also, I think the newest generation, that is, people currently in their 20s, are behaviorally more fluid than we were. They don't believe in labels to the same extent we did. Usually, a minority sets the tone for how we view a given generation. And I think the minority that's setting the tone today for the newest generation, people in their 20s, are much more relaxed. I mean, all the polls that I see in reaction to questions like gay marriage indicate they throw up their hands and say, "What's the big deal? Who cares?" There are so many other issues that are more important. I find great hope in that reaction.

By more important, do you mean larger social justice issues around the economy, the growing concentration of wealth?
Yes.

In the gay community, white men, a few women, still define class issues. Let's take New York City Mayoral candidate Christine Quinn's position on paid sick days, minimum wage. Although now tempered, she started out against adding sick days to low paying jobs as an olive branch to the business community. How could her position have helped a lesbian couple, or any couple, with kids to raise and who work more than two jobs?

91

I haven't talked to anybody who is gay or lesbian who is voting for Christine Quinn. Now, that may reflect the circles I travel in. My friends tend to be political and radical, and they consider Christine Quinn, at best, a centrist. They're almost all voting for Bill de Blasio, the city's official Public Advocate. A lot of these people are older, maybe not as old as I am but they're not in their 20s. They are people who grew up with stricter political definitions than maybe others who are in their 50s or 60s, who might automatically vote for an openly gay candidate. In my circle, they're voting for the candidate who comes closest to sharing their politics.

Does this change in voting habits signal maturation within our own community? To consider policies, not people?
I think it does. It's an awareness that simply because a candidate shares your sexual orientation, or same gender, that that person is automatically kin to you. I mean they're not. You and the candidate may be at loggerheads in regard to many other aspects of being alive.

Class differences come into play, not only shared sexual identities? Will assimilation blunt or sharpen the class differences within the LGBT community?
Some of it depends on how you define class. If you define it in terms of income, job status, level of education, whatever, assimilation is not going to help those people who are at the lower economic rungs of the ladder. I mean many gay people, which the organized gay community doesn't seem to be aware of, are not only working class but are part-time employees who

are living at or below the poverty level. And you'd never know from the agendas of our national organizations that these people mattered because our agendas don't address their issues.

Like the Human Rights Campaign?
The Human Rights Campaign manages to get comfortably affluent gay people accepted, but that's not going to help those who are economically marginalized. And it's not simply about economics. But also race. Currently I just finished working on a manuscript I'm tentatively calling *The Battlefield of AIDS* which is essentially a dual biography of activist Michael Callen and Black poet Essex Hemphill, but it covers the whole period. I knew them both slightly, but only slightly. Callen was an outsider even in relation to the AIDS movement. I mean, he was active very early. He and Richard Berkowitz are sort of the granddaddies of safe sex guidelines. But in terms of ACT UP, Callen was more radical in his *lived* politics. Even though ACT UP, as part of its founding principles, talked about racial equality and gender equality, in practice they had committees like the Minority AIDS Committee and a women's caucus. And the politically radical elements in ACT UP migrated to those committees. But the guiding spirit of the organization was the Treatment and Data Committee, people like Peter Staley and Mike Harrington, who eventually formed the Treatment Action Group, which is still in existence.

And thus far the history of those years is mostly focused on all those fine looking, upstanding white men, all of whom, except for Spencer Cox, survived. And why not? Everybody fights for his or her own life. Who can blame these guys? I don't blame them. It's just that they don't represent all of what was going on in those years of the early AIDS struggle.

Callen and Hemphill both died of AIDS, but they were not TAG types at all. In fact, they were antagonistic to ACT UP. There is more story yet to be told about those years. Essex, for example, would have nothing to do with the organized gay movement, ACT UP or otherwise, because it was so white oriented and dominated. Essex and most minority gays were not not interested in the primarily white gay political movement of ACT UP.

They didn't participate in ACT UP or Treatment Action Group or all of the groups that spawned to do good work?
ACT UP did do good work, lots of it, but it centered on its constituency—middle- and upper-class white men primarily.

More than three decades later, the CDC says if current trends continue 50% of African-American men who turned 18 in 2009 and have sex with men will be HIV+ by age 35. Fifty-four percent of all men who have sex with men will be HIV-positive. Thirty-two years later we still have 50,000+ new infections a year.
I think there are various explanations. Many younger people have bought into the notion that HIV is a manageable disease. To some extent it is. Drugs that control the virus now exist, and many HIV+ people are living normal life spans. But the problem is we don't yet know about the long-term effect of those

drugs. We don't know their natural history. There's enormous individual variation in how the drugs work for each individual. A lot of people don't get tested, I mean a *lot*. I don't have the figures for you, but I know I've read it innumerable times. They don't want to get tested. (CDC: In 21 cities across the country, second and third tier cities, 20% of young gay men, 18 to 36, are HIV infected, most of them young men of color, and 44% don't know they're infected.)

Your friend Sarah Schulman's work has recently focused on "homo-nationalism" or "pink washing" as a theme, based on the work of theorist Jasbir K. Puar. Essentially the idea is that we tend to evaluate Western democracies based on their level of LGBT civil rights. The more incrementally LGBT people become assimilated, and accepted for a place at the table, the less willing they may be to criticize their nation's other policies – about war, the economy, and the civil rights of other oppressed groups within their own nation and in other countries. They fear their hard-fought-for rights may somehow be revoked if they don't tow the line.

I agree with her that's one of the costs of assimilation – along with denying your own specialness, and what it is that you *truly* have to contribute to the mainstream society. With assimilation there is pressure to become a good, upstanding, patriotic American, meaning, for example, if Israel is our "greatest ally" you're expected to support *everything* the Israeli government does. And a lot of what Israel is doing is not okay. I applaud Schulman for bringing all that up.

Is the idea that queers should resemble the dominant, heterosexual culture – get married, raise kids, join the Armed forces – a lingering remnant of internalized homophobia?
Yes, I believe so. We're accepted to the extent we manifest mainstream values. *And* express our gratitude for being allowed in.

In other words, perhaps one aspect of assimilation plays out like "How could I be so rude to object"?
Right. Being rude enough to point out some of the negative features of our own country – like the appalling class structure, the lack of access to health care and education, the huge disparity of income between the top 1% and everyone else.

In your writings, you mention special gay experiences. Are gay people shaman? Some among our thinkers and writers believe we are. That we are capable of perceiving the world in ways that are different from the mainstream and therefore useful to others.
Well, I don't like the word shaman because it connotes spirituality and I'm an utterly secular type. I wish I had the belief gene, but I don't. Whatever it is, I didn't inherit it, gene or otherwise. But leaving aside the term shaman, I do feel that because gay people have had a different historical experience, we have a different perspective on mainstream institutions, a different set of attitudes, even a different set of – what to call it – not habits, but maybe social structures. I don't want to overplay this, but you know there's a real analogy to be drawn with Black Americans. The same sort of dialogue is also going on and has long gone on within the Black community: Do we

really want to become whites or pseudo whites? What are the costs of assimilation? As James Baldwin put it, 'Why do we go on begging to rent a room in a house that's burning down? Why don't we build a better house?' And I think it's exactly the same dialectic that's going on in LGBT circles right now. For example, the Log Cabin Republicans drive me nuts because they accept mainstream values at face value as if they embody truth. They don't. You've got to be a historian of the United States, as I am, to know just how often we have deviated from the mottos that we emblaze on our banners. Our history of imperialism alone dispels the notion that we are the "most humane" of nations.

The myth of American exceptionalism?
Right. But going back to the other point, I think more gay people need to acknowledge that we have had a different experience growing up and therefore our relationships are somewhat different and our general stance on the world is much more ironic and anti-authoritarian than the mainstream, which believes wholeheartedly in church and state. For example, "camp" is essentially ironic, making fun of established pieties. There are many truths about mainstream America that the mainstream itself doesn't recognize. What bothers me so much is that they'll never recognize what it is that gay people have to contribute by way of special insight if we go on denying that we have any special insights.

What special insights do we have?
Insights into a host of values and institutions – gender, friendship, "family," marriage, monogamy, et cetera, et cetera.

I'm not very hopeful that more gay people will acknowledge, both to themselves and in general, that they've had special experiences, and they may have special insights to contribute. I'm not very hopeful simply because life is short and hard. And what most people want is to feel reasonably comfortable in their environment, which means you go along with what seems to be most acceptable to the most people. You don't want to constantly stand out, constantly contradict, and constantly be the outsider. You want to belong. I think assimilationism is what is going to proceed. I don't think the Sarah Schulmans or the Martin Dubermans are going to win this battle.

Stonewall is a battle won. When you look back on your book about Stonewall is there anything you would write differently? What do you know now that you didn't know then?
I still deeply admire those who immediately stood up and fought back. I admire what originally, initially came afterward in terms of new organizations and new attitudes. I think it all quickly devolved into what I call liberal organizing rather than the original radical organizing. I mean the confrontations; the riots themselves were clearly radical. And The Gay Liberation Front was clearly radical. Then slowly we start the descent into assimilation as our sole concern. And I'm part of that. I don't exclude myself. I was on the original board of The Gay & Lesbian Task Force, and I did have my doubts from the very beginning. I said, you know, what is this exactly? I mean we seem to be working for acceptance on mainstream terms rather than working toward asserting our own specialness. I was uneasy, but I was very much a part of it. So, I'm well aware of

the attractions of assimilation. I mean I'm essentially a middle-class mainstream guy. That's how I was brought up, in suburbia no less. My head is far more radical than my lifestyle.

Has age changed your point of view?
As I get older, I get still more radical. Maybe groups like The Gay & Lesbian Task Force and the Human Rights Campaign are all that one can hope for in a country as basically conservative as ours. If you look back at the history of social protest movements in this country, that's what you see: social protest groups initiated by radicals that then quickly devolve into mere "liberalism" – at best. By "liberal" I mean those who believe we already have the finest set of institutions in the world and the only change needed is marginal. By contrast, "radicals" believe that inequality has become institutionalized and what is needed is a top-to-bottom renovation.

Dr. Martin Luther King Jr. had as much energy for opposing the Vietnam War as he did for racial problems...
And for which he was widely denounced.

...but somehow then the next generation, the Student Non-violent Coordinating Committee (SNCC)...
SNCC was to the left of King, but they self-destructed. Unlike so much of Western Europe, in this country we simply don't have a sustained history of radical protest. We don't even have a sustained history of powerful workers' unions. Therefore, it's very hard to believe that we're going to have the kind of transformative politics needed.

And why would the LGBT movement be any different?

Exactly. No group has ever managed it. And I think the culprit here, and I say some of this in some of the essays in the *Reader*, is that most Americans continue to blame themselves for whatever it is in their own lives that they define as unsuccessful. They tell themselves that if they didn't become "successful," however they define it, they blame themselves, their own personal failings: "I didn't work hard enough. I didn't get enough education; I deceived myself about where my gifts actually lay." But they don't blame "the system."

Nothing larger than themselves can be held accountable?

Right. I think enormous suffering comes with that way of explaining the world. Citizens of Western European nations have managed to blame an aristocracy, a theocracy or a monarchy. If you can blame someone other than yourself at least you can tell yourself you didn't get ahead because there were all these built-in obstacles. I wasn't born into the right family, the right class, whatever.: "There's no way somebody born into my circumstances would ever have gotten ahead. The economic obstacles, the institutional obstacles were simply too great." But Americans don't do that. They turn it all on themselves and their own failings.

SEAN STRUB, *BODY COUNTS: A MEMOIR OF POLITICS, SEX, AIDS, AND SURVIVAL*

Sean Strub (born 1958) is synonymous with so many benchmark events in the LGBTQ and HIV movements. *Body Counts: a Memoir of Politics, Sex, AIDS, and Survival,* describes moments involving Yoko Ono, Warhol associates, Tennessee Williams, Gore Vidal, and New York City royalty. He founded *POZ* magazine and The Sero Project addressing HIV stigma worldwide. Strub produced David Drake's Obie and Dramalogue-award winning play *The Night Larry Kramer Kissed Me,* which ran Off-Broadway for a year, making it one of the longest-running solo shows in New York history. Eventually, Drake and I premiered the play-to-film at a queer film festival I produced in Pennsylvania's state capital of Harrisburg.

We met in 1996 at his first POZ Life Expo, the world's first consumer fair for people living with HIV. Next he announced a national tour alongside then-New York City Mayor Rudy Giuliani. Strub knows electoral politics, serving as Mayor of Milford, Pa. He operated a "Senators Only" elevator as an intern in the U.S. Capital, launching his involvement in national Democratic politics.

In 1990, Strub became the first openly HIV positive person to run for the U.S. Congress. Several years later he faced his own mortality with a body covered in Kaposi's Sarcoma lesions and a skyrocketing viral load. Near death when combination therapy was introduced in 1996, he came back to life Lazarus-style to continue his advocacy. To commemorate POZ magazine's 10th anniversary in 2004, Strub enlisted artist-photographer Spencer Tunick to create one of his "naked installations." On a cold March morning, 85 naked HIV-positive people, including this writer, gathered in the legendary Restaurant Florent, in New York's Meatpacking District. David and Arlene Nelson's award-winning short film *Positively Naked*, documented the event, focused on individual stories of five of the people in the photo shoot.

～ ⁊⁊

In our initial email exchange regarding your memoir, you wrote: "...honesty is what I hope this book will spark a discussion about..." Honest about what? How gay men made their revolution mostly sexual? How the repressive Heterosexual Dictatorship had as much to do with the spread of AIDS as did our own sexual behavior? How gay men's sexual practices and political repression combined to create a perfect storm?

There have been mistruths, half-truths and secrets about the epidemic from the beginning. In hindsight, we can understand why they happened, to some extent, but we can also correct the record and take responsibility for our part in those deceptions.

In the earliest years of the epidemic, many of us were not entirely honest with ourselves, let alone the public, about the degree to which the sexual behaviors of many gay men, myself included, facilitated the spread of disease generally and HIV specifically. Even using the word "promiscuity" in any context concerning AIDS was problematic and risked an accusation of being sex negative or anti-gay. Some of that was surely driven by shame, but much of it was from fear of a backlash or a belief that the truth would further impede the appropriate governmental response. For years, the risk to heterosexuals, particularly heterosexual men, of sexually acquiring HIV was vastly exaggerated, for fundraising and political purposes. We haven't been as upfront as we should have been about how HIV is a disease that is sexually transmitted almost entirely by men; there is only a miniscule number of female to male transmissions.

Proportionally, a small number of female to male transmissions may be the case in the West, but what about places like Asia and Africa?
There is no question but that there are only a tiny number of female to male transmissions in the U.S., probably even fewer than are officially reported because some men lie about risk behaviors concerning sex with other men or injecting drugs. The exact reasons for the much greater prevalence of female to male transmission in Africa remains mysterious, but a vastly higher incidence of endemic infections (that both weaken one's immune system and can greatly facilitate transmission) is one major factor.

Let's be clear. The misinformation and deception during the

early AIDS years concerned more than just gay men.

We weren't just deceiving ourselves, or misleading the broader public, it was also how we were deceived. Many of us bought into the hype of AZT as a miracle drug, for example, only later to learn how many of us were harmed by AZT monotherapy. Yet today, few who were responsible for its widespread and dangerous promotion to asymptomatic people with HIV will acknowledge any responsibility.

As your book was releasing, designer and longtime amfAR board chair Kenneth Cole was asked on Chelsea Handler's TV talk show Chelsea Lately *how he got involved with AIDS research. He answered: "This is, was, like 25 years ago and people weren't talking about AIDS then because stigma was so devastating (and arguably stigma has killed more people than the virus itself has), and the gay community wasn't speaking up, they were afraid to." You took him to task on* Huffington Post.

I think Kenneth Cole knows better, and simply misspoke or exaggerated to make his point about how powerfully stifling stigma was in those days. Unfortunately, he won't correct the record and admit his mistake. His historical revisionism accuses the gay community of not doing enough, implying blame, even though I doubt that was Cole's intent. But to those of us who have spent our lives fighting the epidemic, it is profoundly insulting. It is like telling soldiers 20 years after the war that they didn't do enough because they were afraid.

It also seems to be part of a trend that renders invisible so much of what the LGBT community did in the early years and instead celebrates heterosexuals and famous celebrities who swooped in to save us. I don't mean to diminish the important and often courageous role of various celebrities and heterosexuals, but I also won't stand by while our community's leadership and contribution is ignored, diminished or maligned.

Why is it important that gay men, three and four decades after the Stonewall Riot and HIV/AIDS, finally have an honest discussion about our history?
Everything in the world happens faster and faster, including the rate at which the past is forgotten. I don't think we'll solve the HIV epidemic without learning from our history, particularly when we make the same mistakes again and again. To ignore, hide or forget that history and what we have learned from it is to waste a precious resource. Remembering our history is also a way to honor those who fought, and died, for freedoms we enjoy today, including our survival. This is important, whether we're talking about LGBT rights, the AIDS epidemic or any social justice struggle. For gay men it is perhaps particularly poignant, since we lost so many early in their lives. If we don't remember them, who will? We can't expect Kenneth Cole or others, including younger gay/bi men, to know our history if we don't know it ourselves.

Regarding our own history, in the last couple years we've seen a resurgence in AIDS/HIV narratives −movies like **How to Survive a Plague, Fairyland, United in Anger, We Were There,** *and Perry Halkitis' book on survival and resilience,* **The AIDS Generation.** *Why now?*

Much of the reason we are now in this "look back" moment has to do with the passage of time. We are now more than 15 years from the peak of the dying in the U.S., enough time to enable some perspective and for survivors – with or without HIV – to have adjusted to the new reality of an epidemic that is more like a serious chronic illness than immediately life threatening.

If one looks at the cultural production after the Holocaust – books and films, mainly – reflective works weren't really produced in great number until the early 60s and then increased steadily for the following 15 or 20 years. Once survivors adjust to survival, which doesn't happen overnight, in time they are able to process grief and pain that had been siloed or repressed years before and, in time, begin to feel a greater sense of obligation to witness and share what they experienced. There are fewer and fewer people around who were on the frontlines from the beginning and able to tell what happened; it is important that we document this history or we risk losing it.

With fewer and fewer people around who can tell the story of early AIDS, what are your thoughts on our current narratives? Do they differ from your own perspective?
The films, books, and exhibits that we have seen in recent years have also inspired others to create their own; no one project is going to tell the whole story. The AIDS experience is as diverse as is the experience of living. Randy Shilts' book, *And the Band Played On*, is generally considered a fairly comprehensive history of the early days of the epidemic, but it was written before ACT UP was founded and is written from a San Francisco

perspective, where Randy lived and covered the epidemic for the *SF Chronicle*.

David France's film, *How to Survive a Plague*, focuses on one part of ACT UP and TAG and a handful of individuals. The early days of the epidemic in New York has not yet been documented in detail; I do so to some extent, but not nearly to the degree needed. As important as ACT UP was and is (veteran and new ACT UP activists meet weekly in New York City) – and it was a huge part of my life – ACT UP reflects a different kind of empowerment than that promoted by Michael Callen, Richard Berkowitz, Bobbi Campbell, Dan Turner and the guys who wrote the Denver Principles. In many ways, the ideas preceding ACT UP were more radical and influenced me greatly.

There's another aspect that is important to me. I'm not buying into "we were all heroes" and "we changed the world" and all that stuff. That's just too rah-rah and simplistic; we deserve a more nuanced understanding of those times and how it affected us, what motivated us then and what the outcomes are today.

Many of us saved our own lives, which is obviously important, but the history of AIDS activism for many white gay men stands as a singular accomplishment, often not seen by them in context with any broader social justice struggle. Once they achieved the likelihood of survival, their interest went elsewhere.

AIDS activism in communities of color also dates back to those earliest years, but more often was intersectional from the beginning. AIDS had to find its place within the myriad challenges facing those communities. I don't know any activist of color who I think of as being heavily engaged in epidemic work in the late 80s and early 90s who isn't still heavily engaged in epidemic work, including through organizations focused on poverty, penal system reform, drug policy or other issues.

Many of the heroes I admire the most are people who were never photographed, never quoted, people who went about their day-to-day lives as best they could, helping to feed and care for their friends, neighbors and co-workers who were sick. Some of our activism, like ACT UP's changing of FDA drug approval policies, was also an unwitting partner to a right-wing corporate agenda. We need to own that part of the history as well.

Finally, so much of the history remains incomplete. A lot of people recognize the names of the early gay white men who were AIDS activists, but who knows the women, or the gay men of color? Gay white men had a shared identity and cultural infrastructure that documented and preserved and, often, glorified their history.

One thing we must do is not repeat the mistakes of the past. Do we risk repeating old mistakes? What would you like history to teach us?
The biggest mistake is failing to learn our own history, which is something we need to teach in schools and to young LGBT people. But to speak just in terms of HIV prevention specifically,

many continue to respond to and think in terms of the epidemic that was a few years ago, not the epidemic we have today. We can't use fear as a prevention tool because the consequences of HIV infection today are very different than they were in 1989, yet fear-based campaigns are often most popular with old-timers who are still in terrible pain from what we experienced. We know how awful it was and we are frustrated that others, especially young gay men, seem not to understand this. But that kind of HIV prevention messaging isn't effective and may be counterproductive.

Same for shame-based prevention messaging, which is appreciated by those already engaged in the desired safer behaviors, but for those whose behaviors the prevention campaign is trying to change, shame-based messaging drives them further and further away from that change.

We don't target prevention funding to the communities at greatest risk. Two-thirds of new HIV infections are gay men or MSM; yet only a small fraction of prevention funding is targeted to that community. We know that targeted community-based HIV prevention programs are effective, so why in 2014 isn't that where we are spending the funding?

I recently saw this poster and I thought it was interesting emphasizing the importance of history over nostalgia. I wonder if you might have any thoughts on it as we seem to be entering into a sort of canonizing phase of past AIDS/HIV activism.
I love AIDS Action Now's work, and Sero Project (a group

he founded, ran, and turned over to new leadership in 2024) has worked with a number of their people. The nostalgia essay is right on the mark; I don't think learning from our history is the same as the nostalgic impulse. Both have a role, but the most important thing coming out of AIDS Action Now is the freshness of their approach, and their passion, which I think has had an influence far beyond their organization. Sometimes, especially when I'm speaking on campuses, I meet young activists or people who want to be activists and they make comments that lead me to think they think all the "exciting" work was in years past. I tell them about how, in the late 70s, when I became so politically active and engaged in social justice work, I felt like I had "missed out" and was late to the party on the civil rights and anti-war movements. Initially, my work advocating for a nuclear freeze and against Apartheid and other efforts felt pale compared to these monumental battles in the recent past, which had been glorified and romanticized. I tell those students that the most powerful and important activism is what is in front of them today, that all around them are needs and issues and work that a few years from now will look more important and pioneering and significant than it might seem to them today. The most important activism is what each of us can do today, not what someone else did in years past.

MICHAEL CARROLL: ON HIS NEW SHORT STORY COLLECTION, THE BENEFITS OF A SPARE WRITING STYLE, AND HIS LITERARY INSPIRATIONS

In *Little Reef and Other Stories,* his first collection of short stories, Michael Carroll (born 1965) employs an economy of words that describe characters deeply drawn. We've known people like them. These are contemporary characters "who are stuck in a quagmire of ennui." The collection is also his first book length manuscript and I wanted to learn from him how he puts his writing projects together. His ways of framing stories interested me because we share this: Although I completed 12 college credit hours to earn a Journalism Certificate, neither of us have studied in formal writing programs.

When reading his 12 varied tales on 260 pages, I thought of a sculptor who hones away clay to shape what he wants us to see. That's what Carroll does. He's just writing down the way he views the world, all absurdities noted, none judged.

Andrew Holleran, in his *Interview* magazine review of *Little Reef* notes that in one story the narrator says of the French, "In the realm of unhappiness, they gave the Americans a run for their money." Holleran wrote that it was "A not-surprising comment, since the Michael I came to know is a supreme realist:

a down-to-earth, level-headed observer who sees the humor and bullshit in things – especially the literary life, which is the subject that binds these tales whose locales range from Key West to Manhattan, from rural Maine to suburban Florida."

When I arrived for the interview at Carroll's Chelsea/New York City apartment shared with his husband Edmund White, the door swooped open before I had a chance to knock. There stood Carroll, White, and Keith McDermott, known for his role opposite Richard Burton in Broadway's original production of *Equus*. Workers were banging and hammering away somewhere near us in the hallway and the house cleaner was tidying up the residence. Longtime friends and daily email pals, McDermott and White scurried away for a talk-walk about literature and life. Carroll and I reconvened at a fav coffee haunt of his across the street.

⁓ ⁀

This is your first book length manuscript. How did it come together for you?
I wrote my first novel at age 24, a coming-of-age tale about a gay undergraduate, much like *The Mysteries of Pittsburgh* (1988) by Michael Chabon. The short stories in this collection are all new and written within the last two to five years.

Are your more recent stories the same stylistically as other pieces you've written?
Well, they are different than my work which has appeared in *Ontario Review* or *Boulevard* or *The New Penguin Book of Gay*

Short Stories, and other publications. I've changed my style to shorter sentences, nothing Baroque anymore. That flowery style of writing is over for me.

Where does your 'clean' approach come from?
From Richard Yates (any one of his books, though my favorites are *Easter Parade, Young Hearts Crying, Disturbing the Peace*), his clean style, clear action, he doesn't explain everything

The first sentence of each story is a juicy morsel. Enticing reader's right into the story.
It is fun because that's where a story begins for me, with a single thought made into a sentence. I've given up classical structure in that these current stories do not have a calculated story arc. I'm also not big on motive. I write one sentence at a time, then the next, and allow my creative juices to flow, take the story where it goes. I never have an ending in mind. That happens as I write. When I think the story's over, it's over.

Even though your stories begin spontaneously and develop as you write, do your characters come from memory, fiction, or both?
Like French auto-fiction, I do pull characters and scenes from memory, from real experiences, but I may take the details further than real life did.

Your humor sneaks up on readers. Does humor come to you as you write or do you go back to embellish with funny stuff in a rewrite?

I don't try to answer existential questions, that's for sure. I make my characters say funny things as I write. I may go back and add humorous anecdotes to more fully develop the moment or a scene. But generally, I like to provide readers with "air space" so they can fill in their own thoughts.

Your short stories read like opening chapters of novellas or full-length novels. Have any of your stories grabbed you that way, maybe the beginning of a novel?

I intended the stories to be separate pieces even though they are linked as a character reappears. I also wanted them to be short enough for public readings. Length is not always valued in today's Twitter-length world.

Which writers do you admire?

Women more than men. *The Prime of Miss Jean Brodie* (Muriel Spark) made a real impact. Spark is economical with language, spare with the descriptions and details and heavy on forward movement and action and dialogue.

I love Joy Williams (*State of Grace, The Quick and the Dead,* and the stories in *Honored Guest*). Williams comes in quickly from different angles, never obvious. She's unexpectedly funny in the least expected ways. And spare, not overdone, quickly phrased without too much tired, received language. And, of course, Edmund White. We were married Nov. 8 after being together since 1995.

I want to ask about Edmund, but at the end of our interview.

I wrote most of the stories after Ed got sick. (White has been working through a series of strokes, on leave from Princeton with a possible return next Fall. He recently spoke at the New Orleans Saints & Sinners Literary Conference.) Our relationship is well-rounded. We go on" plot walks" to discuss whatever he's working on at the moment.

I needed his encouragement and support as I developed my writing. I had no fancy writing program experience. Where I may have thought I needed criticism, Ed thought I needed encouragement.

JOHN RECHY: ON THE GAY SENSIBILITY, MELDING TRUTH AND FICTION, AND HIS LITERARY LEGACY

Born erudite, John Rechy (born 1931), has authored 14 novels and three non-fiction works. Raised Mexican-American in El Paso at a time when Latino children were routinely segregated, he was assumed to be Anglo because of his light skin. A teacher "changed" his name from Juan to John.

After appearing as Jesus in a play at age ten, Rechy wrote Shirley Temple a letter offering to be her movie partner. His mother was a big fan of Liberace, who sent her a miniature piano and an autographed photo. In 1978, he insisted to *People* magazine about his now canonized novel *City of Night*, "I didn't write it to titillate." That book brought out the worst and best in reviewers and readers and has been in print ever since its 1963 publication.

Gore Vidal hailed him as "one of the few original American writers of the last century," and Michael Cunningham, one of his former writing students, has called him an author "whose life is almost as interesting, and meaningful, as his work."

He wrote memorable commentary and reviews, published in *Beneath the Skin, The Collected Essays of John Rechy,* for *The Nation, New York Review of Books,* and *The New York Times* and a memoir/fictional narrative *About My Life and the Kept Woman*. His insights often pre-sage what others concluded decades later.

Rechy was at first cautious regarding my request, wanting more information on the ground rules and scope of my questions which he later determined were "very good." He wanted the full scope of his work, and life, to be addressed. We talked about the Great Depression, World War II, the Korean and Vietnam Wars, the tumultuous 1960s, the Stonewall Riots, AIDS, and the assimilation of the LGBT community into marriage and the armed forces.

As a young boy, you stayed inside writing stories. Did you always want to be a writer?
Yes, my desire to be a writer came quite early. Before my teens, about ages 7 to 12,

I had written many stories. Several of them were "retellings" of movies and of my father's opera productions. For example, I retold the story of Madame Butterfly and Carmen. Not intentionally, those "adaptations" were very funny. Madame Butterfly to Lt. Pinkerton: "Guess what? I'm pregnant."

At age 13, I began a novel titled *Time on Wings*, a historical novel about–get this! – Marie Antoinette. It reached about 500 pages before I stopped to move on to grittier subjects: a very sexy expose about high school students. I continued to write from then on, and as editor of my high school newspaper and later of the college magazine, I published quite a few scandalous stories. I was fired as editor of a school magazine for a satirical poem and an article titled "Babbitt Ain't Dead, He Just Went to College." Around the same time, I wrote my first finished novel, *Pablo!*, based on Mayan legends. At one time, Grove wanted to publish it, but I didn't want that very early novel to come out as my "second novel" after *City of Night*. I also wanted to be an artist and created several comic strips which were usually set in earlier times. For a time, I also wanted to act, after I was cast as the boy Jesus at age ten.

How did that come about?

My father had worked in Mexico with the great actress Virginia Fabregas, the Ethel Barrymore of Mexican theater. She had her own touring company which came to perform in El Paso, and they needed a kid for the role of an allegorical Jesus in "El Monje Blanco" – the White Monk by Blasco Ibanez. I got the role with an all-star cast of Mexican actors and actresses. I loved the costume – a rather brief loin cloth. My great scene, the climax of the play, was when I was in the area where my father is a carpenter (circa early A.D.), and on the set are several wooden boards, scattered. My mother, an allegorical Mary, is with her husband, an allegorical Joseph. Some kind of crisis is looming, and my father announces that he has to go away. At that point, I leaned back on some boards on stage that formed a cross, and I spread my arms on it. Then I say to my father: "Me abandonas, Padre?" ('Are you abandoning me, Father?") obviously echoing Jesus on the cross. My father then says: "Ya esta crucificado! ("He is already crucified.") That created loud sobs in the audience. After the first performance, I ran out into the audience in my costume and the ladies, some gentlemen too, reached out to hug and kiss me and continued weeping. That was a great time. When the play was going to be made into a Mexican film with the great Maria Felix as Mary, I was chosen to play the part again; but that would require moving to Mexico which was not feasible for our family. A few years later, when I was still a boy, I wrote Shirley Temple offering myself as her partner in movies. She didn't answer, and so my theatrical aspirations were ended.

It's tempting to be reductive. Does your story about playing Jesus at age ten help to define John Rechy into his adult life?
I hope not, in any religious sense. Oh, God, no! However, performing in a sexy costume and arousing so much "love" – that might have had some influence in my latter years.

In a 1988 LA Times *review of your novel the writer quoted you saying that you were a Texas writer not mentioned on lists of Texas writers; a Chicano writer omitted from anthologies of Chicano writers; a California writer ignored in books about California; and even though excluded from homosexual anthologies you were still known as a 'homosexual' writer. How does your legacy look to you today?*
That has changed dramatically, I'm glad to say, although some hints of "being left out" continue. I've been given PEN-USA's Lifetime Achievement, One Archive's first Culture Hero Award; William Whitehead Lifetime Achievement, the Leal

Lifetime Achievement Award for a Mexican-American writer and West Coast Lambda's Pioneer Award. My writings are now taught widely in universities and colleges – especially *City of Night*, and now *The Miraculous Day of Amalia Gomez*, and some other books of mine.

Several students are writing their PhD's on my work and university conferences hold panel discussions on my books. Okay, so that sounds like bragging. It is bragging, yes, and I do it here because I wasn't always included. Plus, I don't believe in "humility," which most often is an arrogant pose. So, yes, I've overcome a lot of weird prejudice, including from gay flanks, like this: Right after *The Sexual Outlaw* had come out, I was baffled by the hostility from gay folk. I did a reading with Alan Ginsburg in of all places San Francisco, and a whole contingent of gay men walked out on me. I went on reading, and then another contingent walked out. I didn't understand why, except that in *Outlaw*, just out, I was upholding "promiscuity" (I call that "sexual abundance") and that was not, then (1977), "correct." Also, in Los Angeles cruising, I was attacked by a huge man denouncing *Outlaw*. As I rolled away from his violent advances a little queen who witnessed my attack offered, "You can't please everyone!" Another time while hustling, I ignored a drag queen. Angry, she said, "Your muscles are as gay as my drag!" These were weird times.

Some years later at a big writer's conference in San Francisco, things had changed powerfully. And (here goes the bragging, non-humility again) I received two standing ovations while

Edward Albee, who was on the same stage, was booed.

You've written seventeen books – 14 fiction and three non-fictions. How do you view your own body of work?
I'm very pleased with it, my body of work. I've ranged very widely, too, both in subject and in form. Gay subjects, yes; but also a Mexican woman in L.A. (*Amalia*), teenagers in Texas (*The Fourth Angel*), a possible daughter of Marilyn Monroe, a spooky female evangelist (*Bodies and Souls*). In my essays, starting back in the 50s, I've written about discrimination against Mexicans in Texas, illegal jailing of "juvenile delinquents," GIs protesting the Vietnam War, and, of course, about the scourge – physical and psychological (on all of us) of AIDS, in *The New York Review of Books*, the *Advocate*, other publications. I want these books, and my essays, to be considered in dealing with my "body of work." I'm glad to say that it increasingly is, and I often speak in classes where one or another of my books is required reading. There are new translations regularly of my work, in Bulgaria just recently.

I think your collection of essays Beneath the Skin, The Collected Essays of John Rechy, *written over 40 years for* The Nation, New York Review of Books, *and* The New York Times *is profound, then and now. With your writing – is there a gay sensibility?*
Of course, there's a gay sensibility. There's a whole essay in my book about that ("Hollywood and Homosexuality: Heterosexual Films in Drag"). And it's a good "sensibility" – we are shaped by exile, born into the "heterosexual camp"

with all that implies. Very early, we deal with "camouflage" in various ways, and that shapes a unique "sensibility." I uphold our differences and resent them being "erased."

You always wanted to be a contender. Are you a contender in the pantheon of gay male writers?
The pantheon of gay male writers? Really, is there such? Do you mean, then, Proust, Wilde, Genet, Djuna Barnes, Virginia Woolf, et. al.? I do think all writers should aim for the best, always; and, yes, that is where I have always aimed. When I referred to myself as a "contender," I meant I simply want my work to be read without prejudice or preconception. Some "critics/reviewers" clearly haven't read my books and still criticize them; it is always easy for a writer to tell when a "reviewer/critic" has not read one's book(s). I don't want to be "corralled" – I want to be viewed as a writer, period.

Related to that – "pantheon" – are the silly lists that purport to indicate a "best," et cetera. those lists are ubiquitous, from *Time* magazine to – yes, really, in my opinion, the bombastic self-appointed guru of literature, Harold Bloom. I feel that those lists and gradings are insulting to artists, I feel, an arbitrary comparison is made, very often reflecting only their personal choices.

Critic/author Jameson Currier wrote in the April 2, 1999, New York Blade News: "Perhaps more than any other American author in the 20th century, his (Rechy) writings have helped shape the sexual consciousness of several generations of gay

men." How has the gay consciousness changed since your early
novels? For better or worse?

I marvel at the folks who have brought up all sorts of
discrimination cases to the courts and fought and won. They're
real heroes. Although we don't see them being invited to ride
as marshals or whatever during our ghastly, giddy parades. I
do hope my books have contributed to good causes. About gay
parades: I think they are entertainment for straight folks. Lots
of moms bring their kids: "Look at the gays, Sonny." I think that
sort of thing should be left for Halloween or New Year's, and
pride parades should be designed with dignity, and I mean all
factions, men in leather, yes, queens in drag, yes, all our factions,
but all produced with pride, not giddiness for heterosexuals to
be entertained or have a chance to laugh at us. In San Francisco,
there is an open "fair" once a year where some of the worst
excesses of S&M are mimed as tourists gather, watching us
whipping, getting whipped, dragged, forced down. Very ugly
entertainment for straight people with their cameras to show
aghast neighbors, laughing.

On being reduced, historically, gay men were defined as
sinners, mentally ill, or criminals. In your essay **The Outlaw**
Sensibility: Liberated Ghettos, Noble Stereotypes, and a
Few More Promiscuous Observations *(1991), you write that*
adopting the outlaw identity "might lead us into a frightening
trap." Please explain.

An extremity of "difference" – emphasize "extremity" – might
veer toward the criminal as quintessential "outlaw." I think Genet
is there. Some gay writers have had a fascination with criminals,

e.g., Capote, Vidal (of course Mailer, but he's not gay).

You've said: "I was always an outlaw except now I want to live."
As a Mexican and a homosexual, you navigated two unrelenting
worlds – the American class system, which we routinely deny
even exists, and the Heterosexual Dictatorship. Was your first
identity as an outlaw tinged with self-doubt?
No, I didn't think of myself as being easily defined, and I have
always rejected self-doubt. As I've always said, I shun "humility"
as a fake pose. I wince when someone receives an award,
especially an Academy Award but also the office of President
or an honor and dutifully – yes, dutifully – mouths the words
"I am humbled." No honor, no recognition, no award should
humble anyone; it should elevate, not only the recipient but
whoever is extending that honor, a grand synergy.

My situation in regard to racial and sexual prejudice is somewhat
unique. In Texas, when I was young, discrimination was quite
powerful against Mexicans, and, of course, Black folk; but I
suppose because my father was Scottish and born in Mexico,
I was fair skinned and so could easily "pass" as Anglo. That
exposed me to hearing terrible insults about Mexicans that I
then rebutted. In the little Texas town of Balmorhea, where I
went with two Anglo friends who were, without knowing I was
Mexican and poor, "rushing" me for their all-white fraternity.
We had dinner at the ranch home of one of my friend's relatives,
a rich woman. At dinner, as we were served by the Mexican
maid, the relative slapped her silver down until the woman
was out of sight, and she announced that the maids had strict

instructions they were to disappear as soon as they served. "I just can't eat when they are around," she said. I think that was what "radicalized" me. I got up and told her that I had to leave her table, then.

And then later you wrote about racism for various publications?
My first published writings in the 1950s were about discrimination and the outrages perpetrated. I was writing about racism for the *Texas Observer*, *The Nation*, and *Evergreen Review*. As a gay man, I didn't experience personal discrimination that I remember; but, of course, I was aware of it and wrote a lot about the subject, including for *The Advocate* and *The New York Review of Books*, along with very early articles about the mysterious illness AIDS. Of course, my book *The Sexual Outlaw* was overtly political in its defense of gay sex, its exposure of vice arrests. I was arrested three times in Los Angeles by vice cops, and I wrote about what happened during those arrests, and after one such article, I was exposed to being tracked by plain clothes cops and assaulted. That sort of thing still goes on, but young gay people don't want to know about that part of our history. It seems that many of them prefer to exist in a limbo, where AIDS doesn't happen, where violence is over. Maybe not all young gay males but too many.

You have stated: "The autobiographer is the biggest liar for claiming: This is exactly how it happened. The biographer is the next level down for arguing: I am capable of knowing another's life. The most honest writer is the novelist, who says: This is a lie, a fiction, but I'm going to try like hell to make you believe it's true." Where do you fall, using your own claim?

I believe what I've said very firmly. I'm not saying that the writer deliberately falsifies, although that is often true, but that memory when applied to an autobiography is entirely unreliable. Yet autobiography is often accepted and attempted as "the truth." The past constantly changes in our memories – memory is a harsh editor. About biography: I read a long time ago Stefan Zweig's biography of Marie Antoinette (when I was writing my own "Marie Antoinette" novel), and in one place he wrote that during her marriage night the curtains that enclosed the royal bed did not move – meaning the couple didn't have sex. That stopped me. How the hell did he know that?

I've been moving into a melding of "true" (i.e., remembered) autobiography and fiction. In *About My Life and the Kept Woman*, I melded the two – biographical events and their transformation into "fictional narrative." In my new book, almost finished and titled *Island! Island!* I use autobiographical events from years ago when I was a guest at a private island. Within the book itself, the narrator begins writing the novel he may write based on those events. I call it "a true fiction."

You've taught creative writing. Michael Cunningham (The Hours) and Kate Braverman (poet, novelist) studied with you before their careers began. Care to share memories?

Only this: That it pleases me enormously that my first encounter with their work was in my writer's workshop. I recognized how uniquely talented each was. Michael remains a friend, and Kate and I became friends, and we played Scrabble;

she was very good, but – she may say otherwise – I usually beat her. Of course, there have been many other well-known writers that have emerged from my workshops. My mate, Michael, who studied with Stella Adler, told me this story about her: In a new class, she was asked what it was like to know that she had "taught/mentored" the likes of Marlon Brando, Meryl Streep, and Robert De Niro. She answered that, yes, her experience with them was good; but that she powerfully lamented those who were equally talented and never made it. Very wise, very sad. I feel the same way. I've encountered in my workshops (at Occidental College, UCLA, USC, and my private workshops) hugely talented writers who have not yet "made it." I try everything I can to bring them attention but at times "The Great Stupid Out There" does not budge.

Author/critic Michael Bronski has said about you, "(He) super-radically and forever altered how mainstream American culture wrote about, saw, experienced, and conceptualized homosexuality..."
That's really good, but I don't know how exactly that is so; but I admire Mr. Bronski a lot, and if he said so, then it's true. In the arts, aside from writers, David Hockney, Gus van Sant, others; and, ironically, several heterosexual figures have acknowledged my influence, including David Bowie, Jim Morrison, Tom Waits, Soft Cell, Bob Dylan.

The following pleases me and amuses me: The opening lines of The Village People's iconic disco hit *YMCA* are clearly inspired by an early chapter in *City of Night*, where the "youngman" protagonist is directed to the YMCA by, of all people, a cop. The song refers to that and refers to "youngman" as a compound word. What I like is that that song is routinely sung now at heterosexual weddings. The Village People, unlike the others, have never acknowledged the origins of their inspiration.

You've created a signature style that combines words – youngman, sexturf, sexhunting. How did that device come about?
I love words and some words when combined create different meanings. I must say, too, that a big misunderstanding about me that came about from those combined words is that I was not that bright. Can you imagine that?

Mainstream gay America is now about marriage and military service. Progress, or is assimilation acquiescence to heterosexual norms?
Wonderful, terrific progress! But also, just as much a dangerous, psychic time for us were we risk losing our unique qualities, our differences, our rich sexuality, our gay "sensibility." I hope we will never become "straight imitators." When I hear married gay males referring to each other as "husbands," and lesbians referring to each other as "wives" I wince. I wince when I see the giant white wedding cakes, and the tuxedos. It is offensive to me because it makes it seem as if what we wanted all along were all the giddy and silly trappings of straight marriage. Okay, look, I never celebrated marriage, gay or straight; however, we saw the brutalities that occurred during the AIDS crisis when long-time partners were denied being with their dying partners. Yes, achieving marriage status is important for us because of

the reality of inheritance, taxes, lots of good stuff not possible otherwise. That to me is all that's important about achieving "marriage." Those benefits have an exigent reality. The day before no more marriages would occur in Los Angeles, Michael and I were driving past the judicial building where the licenses were being given out. It was then that we thought, it's important, let's go do it. We were told we were too late in the day, but we managed to charm the lovely Black lady and a Chicana rooting for us, and so they went ahead and gave us the certificate. Then the Black lady said she'd perform the wedding, and, in her impressive robes, she led us to a small room decorated in white for weddings. Michael and I stood before the lady in her elegant robe – and I hesitate to tell you this because it is so extremely romantic and even sentimental, Michael and I were both moved, very much. Yeah, we held hands – she told us to – and kissed – but that wasn't the reason we did it. We did it because, well, yes, it was quite lovely.

And I do hope that being married doesn't mean that we will adopt the nonsense restrictions of hetero marriages; like rigorous demands of so-called "fidelity." I'm not sure either that the form courtship has taken among gay men is going to work. I mean, to me, it is unnatural for gay men to date first and get to know each other before they have sex later, if at all. It's more natural for us as gay men to follow the old-fashioned way: Have sex (protected sex, of course), don't talk a lot before or during sex – then, if something significant remains after the (protected) sex, like good feelings, possible bonds of interest, good conversation, then date each other.

Sarah Schulman has written extensively about "homo-nationalism," coined by Rutgers professor Jasbir Puar in her book Terrorist Assemblages. *The phrase means that the benevolence of Western democracies is judged by LGBT advances, namely marriage and military service. She fears assimilation at the big table means LGBT folks will grow less inclined to challenge, for example, if the Iraq Wars were necessary or if the state has compelling interests in allowing religious exemptions to gay marriage. Your thoughts?*

I, too, am apprehensive about assimilation, and borrowed celebrations after gay weddings (giant cakes, balloons, all the props of straight weddings). Like I've said I hope we never become "straight-impersonators." I was in the army, the 101st Airborne Infantry Division. And in the army gay men were pretty open back in the 50s and 60s. I thought, really, it was a good thing that you could get out of the hated "services" by revealing that you were gay. Of course, you had to pay a price for that – dishonorable discharge, benefits withheld. I'm talking more metaphorically here. Of course, gay people should be able to join the army, whatever, even be a cop, I guess. I do hope that gay people will always be at the forefront questioning unjust heterosexual authority like the criminal Iraq War waged through lies about weapons of mass destruction. I hope that since we have been the objects of massive injustice, we would be among the first to question it elsewhere.

The labels we choose for ourselves change as our circumstances change. But you don't like "gay" as a moniker?

Now I marvel at what gay people choose to call themselves.

"Gays" still makes me wince, and I remember Christopher Isherwood saying that made us sound like "bliss ninnies" and so it does; too late to change that. I am sad to know that lesbians are abandoning their grand designation", the classy designation of "Lesbian." But the worst development is accepting the word "queer." That's crazy. The word is ugly, the meaning is ugly. For gay men I have often suggested we call ourselves "Trojans."

Did you know Gore Vidal? How did you interact with him?
Although people assume I knew Mr. V., I never met him. We "saw" each other twice. In his *Paris Review* interview years back and in his Forward to a book of his essays, he made nasty remarks about me, while having claimed that he never "struck first." He did, quite often. I wrote to him protesting his swipes at me, and he wrote back very nearly apologizing; my agent's wife does claim that's the only time he actually did apologize.

When I was much younger, I admired Mr. V., his courage, his essays (brilliant at times); but as I learned more about him – especially his view of hustlers, how he underpaid them, his disdain, his chintziest – my admiration began to wither. His granting all the money from his estate to Harvard – not a cent for legitimate gay causes, e.g., AIDS/cancer research, money to help elderly gay men and lesbians. Also, his bullshit about "no homosexuals, only homosexualists, only homosexual acts" was repulsive, his own definition to allow him to continue in the closet, peeking out now and again, then dashing back in – in intellectual camouflage.

Responding to my objection to certain homophobic attitudes in *The New York Review of Books*, he wrote to me that he felt the same and therefore would never again write for that periodical. Of course, he continued to write every month or so. What remains, for me, is this: The superb essays, the prose, the wit. Oh, yes, he was mighty arrogant. When he was living in Los Angeles, he got a friend of mine and his – the wonderful writer Gavin Lambert – to call me to ask whether I would like to come to lunch with them at his home. It was 11:30 A.M. and he was inviting me to lunch! That was insulting. Of course, I didn't go. I have to say that I regret this change in my view of him. I truly admired him, highly, for several decades.

You provided your perspective on Vidal to Tim Teeman for his biography In Bed with Gore Vidal...

I wondered, and said so to Teeman, as did many of Vidal's friends and peers, what underpinned his desire to remain undefined, as not "gay" per se. I found him "fascinating. For all his bravery and courage, which he had in spades, he never came out. He did not want to be identified as a homosexual. In an incredible way he was trying to define homosexuality in a way to fit him perfectly: a mode of never really coming out or this empty bisexuality, which people doubted. He was (uncomfortable) with overt "homosexuality."

At the end of About My Life, you recall how, reluctantly, you wrote City of Nights. Why reluctantly?

I never intended to write about the streets and hustling. What happened was that during Mardi Gras in New Orleans, I went somewhat crazy, booze, pills, sex, and more sex, no sleep – and in the madness of Mardi Gras (as if heaven and hell had opened up and sent everyone out screaming into the dirty streets), I saw myself sinking, losing myself; for the first time I doubted that I would ever be a writer. I saw a bleakness ahead. I fled back home to El Paso, my mother's house in the projects. There I felt lost, terrified really. I wrote a letter to a friend about my experiences in New Orleans.

I didn't send the letter, I thought I had thrown it away. About a week later I came upon it, and it sounded like a story. I sent it to *Evergreen Review* and lied by saying it was part of a novel "almost finished." My great editor Don Allen saw through the lie but championed my work. I only then began to write in sections. Slowly, I thought, yes, it could be a novel. But as I wrote it and even now, I often feel a terrible sadness, as if I had betrayed the queens and the hustlers, and the customers. I had lived among them and now was leaving. I do tell myself that as characters they do continue to live. But I am often haunted by memories of the real people that I wrote about, and wonder where they might be; like Miss Destiny, Chuck the Cowboy, Mr. Klein, who were living on the edge.

Your novel **Rushes** *(1979) profoundly presages the next immediate chapters in the lives of gay men, in some ways on the edge. It mimics New York City's The Mineshaft and sex venues like it during the Stonewall-to-AIDS years (1969-1981). You had gay men in mind when writing it?*
I told the *LA Times* in 1988 about *Rushes*: "I just didn't aim

Rushes at the gay community. In a way we were reaching a dead end… And although I had been a champion of sexual liberation, I had seen some of the bludgeoning of it, some of the dangers that were occurring."

No one can claim to have "foreseen" the invasion of AIDS; no one. But what was happening just before that was the exclusivity of sex, the proliferation of violent sex – yes, the Mineshaft. I think what was occurring was an actual bludgeoning of our senses. Nothing was enough. So-called "fisting" became a sexual act. There were the toilets, the filthy bathtubs, slings, imported garbage, jail cells (how many of us experienced the actual ones), and much more. Intimate sex with one partner was not enough – there had to be three, four, five, more and more. In *Rushes*, the protagonist looking at the orgy downstairs, thinks that what he sees looks like a huge animal devouring itself.

By the late 70s, early 80s, was every aspect of the 60s counterculture devouring itself? Did putting all our energies into sexual liberation only advance or retard efforts of the larger culture to understand gay men?
I think you state it very well. We had reached a dead end. Nothing was enough, and because of that we were pushing gay sexuality into a place where it wasn't sex any more. It had become, often, pain and humiliation. I'm not talking about our rich proclivity for sex, often called "promiscuity." As long as sex is protected and allows for human contact, that is, feelings, I see no terrible negative.

*Was the whole Mineshaft experience an elaborate acting out of
Catholic guilt intertwined with internalized homophobia?*
I structured *Rushes* as a Catholic Mass, very carefully. The
description of the bar makes it very like a church. The graffiti on
the walls correspond to the Stations of the Cross but rendered
as gay pornography. The last station, which is cloudy in Catholic
dogma, I turned into a tangle of lines, disintegration. The S&M-
er Chas has dialogue that begins with "I believe ..." – and then I
followed the rhythms of the credo, but, here, Chas is "believing
in the rituals of S&M. When the action descends to the lowest
level of, yes, the Mineshaft, there is a mimed crucifixion – and
outside there is gay-bashing. To me the connection with the
bloodiness of the Mass and the rituals of S&M are related. I
know I've become controversial because of my views on S&M.
I talk about that from experience, from my own participation.
I see it now as miming not only religious violence ("As often
as you shall do these things in memory of me shall you do
them" – it couldn't be clearer), but ourselves enacting a ritual
of self-hatred, including both the so-called "master" and the so-
called "slave" – and how often the roles are reversed. Handcuffs,
chains, those are the real props cops use on us during arrests,
and so we play-act at that. I would never suggest those rituals
be "banned" or forbidden as rituals of our oppression; I have
always suggested only looking into those rituals honestly. Now
I'm not talking about role-playing at control or submission or
just wearing leather – I'm talking about the heavy rituals of
pain and "slavery" and real humiliation.

Look. A few years ago, there was in Los Angeles a "gay slave auction" – with all the trappings, handcuffs, chains, et cetera. It was raided by L.A. cops. There was this revealing spectacle: Fantasy masters and slaves were handcuffed and carted off to jail by real cops. I've been arrested three times, and I can tell you that real handcuffs and jail cells are nothing to play at. Too ugly, too serious.

Where does all the S/M come from? In his movie **Sex Positive** *Richard Berkowitz, himself a former hustler, opines that New York City's gay sex culture, and other urban centers, had unknowingly absorbed negative tensions about gay sex from the larger culture.*

I think that masochism is at the core of the Christian religion, especially since that's what I was as a kid, in the Catholic Church. The main symbol is, of course, Christ on the Cross, suffering, bleeding, dying. But he is also very sexual – the long loincloth on the almost-naked body, the striated muscles, the beautiful face. And look: The contortions might even be seen as sexual, "coming." Suffering and sexuality, especially when stupidly prohibited, become paired. It's that suffering (or coming) figure that congregants kneel before. Pretty S&M-y, no? And I do believe that in the name of religion that more outrages than from anything else have been perpetrated over and over throughout history.

You've held, maybe still hold, radical views. When **The Sexual Outlaw: A Documentary** *sold out its first printing you said, "public sex is revolution, courageous, righteous, defiant revolution." Still believe that? Or were your words contextual* *to the times?*

Yes, contextual. AIDS changed that, and then so did the computer. Essentially, I still celebrate the richness of gay sexuality – cruising, making out, all that, but always, always employing safe-sex. It is frightening to read that HIV instances have become dramatically less among heterosexuals, but that among, especially, young gay men, infection has increased dramatically.

I don't know how that figures into "internet" meetings for sex. As long as the sex is protected or safe, that would not seem to be a factor in HIV's proliferation.

To deviate: About "sex on the internet" – especially porn – it amuses me the number of males who identify as "gay for pay." I think a more accurate description would be "straight for pay." And by that, I mean pretending to be "straight." Back in the day, when I was hustling, clients would often demand: "You're not gay, are you?" A bold affirmative answer might very often cancel any arrangement. That, too, of course, is a form of self-hatred, isn't it?

The theme in your novel Marilyn's Daughter *is that we cannot run away from ourselves. If we remake ourselves, we start with who we are and then move to who we wish to be. Are you finally where you want to be? At 83, are you finished?*

Finished! You mean through? Ended? Over with? Gone to get my reward? If so, no, not at all. I'm finishing my novel, *Island! Island!*, deep into another one, and planning a third. My mate

Michael, a successful Hollywood producer, and I are closer than ever. He's a miraculous relationship I never sought or expected. It just happened. We live in a beautiful home in the Hollywood Hills. I continue to work out with weights, and although the word "love" makes me cringe, yes, our wonderful love has endured and grown for, now, for almost 40 years. I sometimes say that instead of committing suicide, I met Michael, and my life changed.

Now, I think a lot about my literary work. I hope that eventually the restrictive labels I've been burdened with – Chicano writer, gay writer, Los Angeles writer will become simply "writer." I am very proud of my work, its wide range, and I want to see it evaluated on its intended level, as literature. And so, who am I now? I'm someone who's lived fully, even when sad, and I am a combination of all I have been. I guess that's a bit of a "lofty" answer, but truly, I've never subscribed to the "finally–discovering-who-I-am" thing–a kind of false epiphany, I think, something that authors are fond of saying they're after. This is a mangled "paraphrase" from Becket; but I'll go ahead and mangle it: "I can't go on, I won't go on, I must go on."

FELICE PICANO: ON REMEMBERING THE PAST, THE AIDS CRISIS, AND GAY ACTIVISM

Felice Picano is the author of more than thirty books of poetry, fiction, memoirs, nonfiction, plays, and several national and international bestsellers. His work has been translated into many languages. Continuing his prolific output since this 2015 interview, Picano edited a second *Best Gay Romance* series. The following year he released the story collection *The Tapping at Cranburgh Grange*. There's more. The sleepless author also produced three novels: *Justify My Sins* (2019), *Pursuit* (2021), and *Lillian's Story* (2022). Finally, his epic *City on a Star* trilogy began with *Dryland's End* (new edition 2021), carried on with *The Betrothal at Usk* and concluded with *A Bard on Hercular*.

His popular books *True Stories Too: People and Places from My Past* and *Nights at Rizzoli* deal with his old New York City haunts, family, friends, and lovers – and, in *Rizzoli*, readers learn about Salvador Dalí, Jerome Robbins, Jackie Onassis, Gregory Peck, Mick Jagger, S. J. Perelman, I. M. Pei. Philip Johnson, Josephine Baker, and John Lennon, who all shopped at the legendary bookstore when Picano worked there. He provides readers intimate access to the private and cultural lives of his times.

My absolute favorites are Picano's well researched *The*

New York Years: Stories by Felice Picano (2000) *and Art and Sex in Greenwich Village: A Memoir of Gay Literary Life After Stonewall* (2007). The territory covered represents my years in what was then called The Big Apple. As I've written in *Crashing Cathedrals: Edmund White by the Book* (2019): Until recently, and certainly before and immediately after Stonewall, the Heterosexual Dictatorship was in full control of the culture. Picano's New York-based allows readers to sample those times from afar.

"It's a good interview I can stand next to," Picano emailed upon his interview's publication.

The late comedian Mitch Hedberg once joked, "One time, this guy handed me a picture of him, he said, 'Here's a picture of me when I was younger.' Every picture is of you when you were younger." After writing about your earlier years, what appears the same/different about yourself?

When I began writing memoirs in the early '80s, I was already aware that I was not the person I had been at 11 or 14 or 19-years-old. As I get older, I'm coming to realize that I've had eight or nine lives already – like the cat whose name I share. The Felice Picano of the Jane Street years, or the one of the Violet Quill Club era, or of the Gay Presses of New York period, or even the first decade living in L.A., is only partly who I am now. I cannot truly know who that person was again since I'm no longer living his life. A friend recently sent me a video interview Vito Russo did with me in the mid-80s for his TV program then and I waited a long time before watching it out of fear that I would come off as a total jerk. But I was surprised when I watched how professional and together this younger version of me actually was. I am sufficiently distanced to appreciate that.

Speaking of distance, Aeschylus said, "Memory is the mother of all wisdom." What wisdom has your impeccable memory taught you?
After seven decades the only wisdom I've arrived at is that life is really hard and that I've had major advantages being born male, white and American. Also, most people really are trying to do what is best, so I should be as kind as I can to everyone, including myself.

Gore Vidal used the word "palimpsest" to describe his memoir, meaning his memory of passages were scraped or washed off like the word's origin so they could be retold. As you have written your own memories, have you used the same technique?
I have a lot of trouble forgetting anything. And in fact, many studies being done on people with "impeccable" memories are now showing that it is actually a physiological fault in the brain that *inhibits forgetting*. So, my memories are definitely not scraped off. Sometimes, they are reordered and easier to live with once I've written about them. Sometimes, they are less of a problem. But they never seem to vanish. The AIDS years especially are filled with so many moments that I cannot ever get rid of. The sounds and odors of someone I deeply cared for in their last minutes alive, for example, are not things that I can ever put aside. But I try to balance all that with wonderful

memories, of which I have many too.

Thinking of memories, you opened the first **True Stories Too** *with: "Look for a long time at what pleases you, even longer at what pains you." What pleases you and what pains you?*

The AIDS Crisis, of course. (Note: Picano knew as housemates the first two gay men on the East Coast to die as the epidemic began.) Nothing else comes close by comparison. It was a period of fourteen years. I'd buried a partner and, as many of us did, asked, "Who's next?" and moved through life caring for and burying friends until there was no one left. But I'm basically an optimistic person. After that stretch of time, I traveled to Japan, spent a year in Berlin (the subject of an essay), and then moved to the West Coast, which is where I've been for nineteen years.

You were friends with Vito Russo and have been critical of how his legacy is presented, especially in his biopic **Vito**. *So far, our histories are about (mostly) white gay men of middle-or upper-class backgrounds. To be fair, these men were movers and shakers, but often to the exclusion of minority men and most women of any demographic. Martin Duberman's* **Hold Tight Gently** *is one exception. Do we have a responsibility when telling our history to mention who was excluded, and why, if we know why?*

I've always tried to include men and women of color in all of my endeavors, simply because I grew up in a multi-colored city, went to a multi-colored high school, was on multi-colored teams, dated an African-American girl in 1960 and have continued to have a wide variety of friends throughout my life.

So, it's more or less natural for me. This also was true during early Gay Liberation years. Isaac Jackson had a program on the New York City official radio station geared toward the Black community, and for several years in a row after Stonewall, he would have me and others on the program the night before the Pride March, and we would urge people of color to show up. For many years, no one ever did. Writer friends of color have told me since that there was a huge disconnect in those years between being Black and being gay. That's a valid explanation. The Ferro-Grumleys and I were part of Black and White Men together at the New York City Gay and Lesbian Center, and out of that grew the Black Heart Collective of writers like Donald Woods, Essex Hemphill (the subject of Duberman's book, along with Michael Callen), Assotto Saint, et cetera. Most of them are long dead and very much missed.

Despite all that, early Gay Liberation in America actually was a 98% white, male, college-educated, middle-class movement. That was the group already radicalized and already trained in protest movements during the 1960s, and also the group that could afford to be arrested and fired from jobs if it came to that. Several gay minority people have subsequently told me that they would have liked to be involved but were just too scared and often too busy just getting by economically. That's completely understandable. But denying what was really going on by saying that early Gay Liberation excluded people of color, or that contrarily it was a "Rainbow," is historically a lie. We're not children, and I believe that history should not be changed to make folks feel better.

You're well-traveled, having visited Iceland, France, Ireland, Germany, Holland, France, Italy, Japan and Australia, and even Istanbul as an openly gay man. At one point in True Stories Too, *a friend tells you how Japan at the time you were lecturing was 20 years behind us on gay rights. How is the U.S. the same and different from other countries?*

I've been so lucky to be able to travel as a writer and as a visiting author; I recommend it to everyone who can afford it to try to do so. In Germany, for example, there are gay bars that have full bars but are also coffee houses. So, you can either go up to the bar, or you can sit at a table in a window area or a more private area. It cuts down the alcohol element and makes it easier to just sit there with a friend or even alone and not feel conspicuous or out of place. They're so much friendlier than our colder stand-and-pose gay bars, which have sent so many guys to Grindr.com.

The dance clubs in Germany are more mixed too. They have guys *and* girls, and straight people come in and feel welcome too. I happened upon an outdoor gay club in Bavaria, too, a real beer-garden, filled with hot guys in lederhosen. I was surprised to find back rooms (i.e., sex rooms) in Reykjavik, Milan, Florence and Marseilles. They're totally taboo in the U.S. these days. And the men in them aren't shy. I was peering into one in Iceland and several arms reached out and pulled me in. Granted, I left before doing anything more than some smooching.

In Japan most of the bars are tiny – about as big as your living room. People buy tickets at the door for X number of drinks, or if they are regulars, they have their own bottle or keg prepaid, and that's what they drink. Scotch and beer are the staples in Japanese gay bars; forget sake. In all of these places, I found a great deal more mixing and openness than in our own gay bars – more of a party atmosphere, especially in the ones that cater to *gaijin*, or foreigners. And the dance clubs – like the huge ones in London and Paris–can seem like American circuit parties one minute, and like a friendly get together the next. Bath houses also vary, from the Apollo Sauna in Berlin, which is a little bit of heaven on earth filled with beauties, to the family-friendly ones in Kyoto, or the "Turkish" baths in Eastern Europe, which have some furtive gay sex going on. In Yokohama, I ended up in a known Yakuza (Mafia) bath house, with hot guys in half-body tattoos and missing pinky fingers.

It seems as if the dead never leave us. **In Another Berlin Story,** **you note that Germans no longer think about World War II's** **destruction.**

I was living in Berlin in the mid-90s, which were half-century commemorative years for the Nazi era and World War II, and some did try to remember and honor the bad past. Also, I was there when *Schindler's List* came out as a movie, and it had a profound effect on German people, to the extent that there were arguments during the film showings leading to fisticuffs, and people in the audience were having strokes and heart attacks. They had to set up First Aid units and oxygen tents in some theater lobbies.

Like war's decimation, the ravages of AIDS in the early years no longer resonate with young gay/bi men, yet rates of infection are astoundingly high within that age group. The fear of death is gone; fear of infection is not. The HIV infection rate among US men who have sex with men is 2.4%. That's high. That means if nothing changes, 40% of gay men by the age of 40 will be infected. If current trends continue, 50% of African-American men who turned 18 in 2009 and who have sex with men will be HIV-positive by age 35.

Recently, the CDC said that all sexually active HIV-negative gay men should consider using Truvada in a prophylactic way (known as PrEP or pre-exposure prophylactic). If indeed Truvada or something similar works, then all of the intellectual and moral issues around the subject, which I've always felt were irrelevant anyway, will simply go away. Should guys then have wild sex as we did in the far past? I don't know: it's an individual decision. But people ought to have the right to make that decision.

True Stories Too: People and Places from My Past *opens and closes with a family story. Has your family been your anchor all these years, in person and in memory?*

By no means. My family has seldom been any kind of a support and has always been a terrific drain on me, emotionally, financially, and in every way you can imagine. I finally escaped their more hideous dysfunction early, at the age of 16, and have lived away from them ever since. I have many Jewish friends, and my partner was Jewish, and they were and are always horrified to hear that despite my high educational achievements, my parents refused to allow me to go to college. So, I left home and

I put myself through college and never looked back and have had as little as I could in dealing with them.

Have the many characters you've chronicled been based on your family?

It is the job of a writer to convey a world that is gone. There are so many different types of people, some well-known and some not known at all. All are good subjects, and all the people who have been around us define who we are. I find them fascinating. I'm the dullest of them.

MICHAEL MEWSHAW DEMYSTIFIES CELEBRATED AUTHOR IN *SYMPATHY FOR THE DEVIL: FOUR DECADES OF FRIENDSHIP WITH GORE VIDAL*

In *Sympathy for the Devil: Four Decades of Friendship with Gore Vidal*, Michael Mewshaw (born 1943) deals with the light and dark of Vidal viewed at close range. Mewshaw and his wife, Linda, first met him in October 1975 in Rome, when Mewshaw approached Vidal to write what became a years-long series of magazine interviews revealing an individual as complex and gorgeous as any of Vidal's historical or fictional characters.

Other than multiple hours of television appearances archived on YouTube, I missed my opportunity to experience Vidal at any range. He's famously quoted as having said: "Never miss a chance to have sex or appear on television." Accounts of his life confirm he kept his pledge. If he was to appear on the late night Jack Paar talk show on a non-school night my mother would alert me with permission to stay up late. Mothers always know? I began my literary love affair with Vidal as an essayist, the genre at which many admirers think he excels. Then came *Kalki*, a 1978 pre/post-apocalyptic novel involving a religious cult that is eerily prescient to the current state of political affairs in our Republic, a form of government Benjamin Franklin wasn't sure we "could keep" given pressures, then and now, to adopt a more regal form of national leadership. The voices in his seven historical novels that cover the entire history of what he calls "The United States of Amnesia," reflect actual conversations drawn from letters, newspapers, and memoirs making each novel a masterpiece of historically documented facts. I cherish my copy of *The Paris Review* 59 in which Vidal says to his interviewer: "Finally, I am proud to say that I am most disliked because for twenty-six years I have been open rebellion against the heterosexual dictatorship in the United States."

I unsuccessfully made my pitch for his time about six weeks before he died July 31, 2012.

Mewshaw unravels for readers many sticky issues around the celebrated writer's life, including White's flare up with Vidal over White's publishing *Terre Haute*, a play with characters based on an imagined series of conversations between Oklahoma City bomber Timothy McVeigh and Vidal.

***

In Sympathy for the Devil: Four Decades of Friendship with Gore Vidal *author Michael Mewshaw reveals an individual as gorgeous as any of Vidal's historical or fictional characters. His portrayal of Vidal is not a bouquet, yet it does reflect the love of a friendship lasting four decades. Mewshaw was in awe of the master, but he was not taken in by him. He and his wife, Linda, first met him in October 1975 in Rome; Vidal had just turned 50 and was financially solid. At the time, the biographer approached Vidal to write what became a series of interviews for* *various magazines.*

Vanity Fair's James Wolcott takes Mewshaw to task for revealing so many of Vidal's shortcomings in a book he says is "dominated by the jagged decay of Vidal's final stage." The biographer explained that that's what his book is about by design: "I'm mostly speaking about Vidal in later life," a life that was troubled and, according to his account, had a long decline. "Seven years after meeting, Vidal told Linda he had contemplated suicide." Vidal was 57 then, 86 when he died.

Counterpoint to his darker side, Mewshaw tells how Vidal – an otherwise barbed tongue who once said, "Every time a friend succeeds, a little bit of me dies" – had a soul. He often helped others on the sly without drawing attention to himself. Vidal was veiled while appearing accessible. The book's first sentence is: "Despite his aloof and at times forbidding demeanor, Gore Vidal managed to project an image that persuaded millions of people around the world that they knew him on a personal basis."

For perspective, Christopher Bram, in *Eminent Outlaws: The Gay Writers Who Changed America*, said about Vidal, among other observations: "I've been reading him since I was a teenager in the 60s and loved reading him, especially his essays. But I realized early that he wouldn't be the kind of guy I'd want to hang out with."

Mewshaw did hang out with Vidal for decades, witnessing drinking habits that brought Vidal to his knees, although it is important to remember that Big Drinking was part of the 20th-century literary scene. Vidal's nemeses Norman Mailer and Truman Capote, as well as his cruising-for-sex pal Tennessee Williams, consumed vast quantities of alcohol, as did Jack Kerouac, whom Vidal claimed in a 1994 interview he screwed in the Chelsea Hotel, where they each signed their own names. In an interview with Martin Amis in *The Sunday Telegraph*, Vidal claimed he left the U.S. "because I didn't want to become an alcoholic," mentioning Fitzgerald, Hemingway and Faulkner as "the classic examples."

A notorious drunk, Vidal's mother Nina eventually married Hugh Auchincloss, as did Jacqueline Kennedy's mother Janet, positioning Vidal and Kennedy to share the same stepfather, but through different mothers. That's not all they shared. Gore's room became Jackie's, and then the First Lady's and John F. Kennedy's for their visits, a fact of life no drag queen could make up. After *Time* published a cover story on her son, Nina sent the magazine a letter "excoriating Gore for ingratitude," insisting she played a crucial role in his career, even setting him up in the film industry. Nina's intercession severed her relationship with Vidal for life. The point is that the demon alcohol was never absent from Vidal's life, but it would be a huge mistake to see him only through that hazy lens.

Beneath the cultivated, hung-over veneer was a man who helped actors secure parts and sent friends money. "Vidal wasn't a conventional friend," Mewshaw says. He wasn't going to show up at your door with a casserole after a trying week.

However, when Vidal put on his bitch cap, one wanted to steer clear. After all, he did say, "It is not enough merely to win; others must lose." Wondering whether he would win or lose, back in 1975, Mewshaw had Vidal's telephone number passed along by a mutual friend. "Vidal didn't so much invite us as summon us to his apartment for drinks."

Perhaps Vidal's pedestrian insecurities, noted by Mewshaw in many scenes, helped him style his "strike first and often" posture. In a 1975 interview with Gerald Clarke in *The Paris Review*, Vidal calculated that the disdain he earned from so many resulted from his creative versatility: "I do many different things rather better than most people do one thing." Later, he laments the fact that "no critic has ever noticed" the theme of *The City and the Pillar*, that character Jim Willard finds all future lovers wanting when compared to his first love. "The novel was not about the City so much as about the Pillar of Salt, the looking back that destroys." Although he swore otherwise to the point of protesting too much, perhaps Vidal suffered the same fate as his protagonist Willard – the fate of always having to look back. This may explain why he doled out details of his fixation with James Trimble piecemeal: "I knew him for 18 years before he ever mentioned Trimble. I think (…) Howard Austen, his partner of 53 years, went 30 years. Lifetime friends went 40," Mewshaw says. Vidal's own divergent accounts, plus the skepticism of friends, have led some to wonder if the ardent love Vidal remembered was imagined with Trimble as his "perfect twin." Was his love for Trimble the defining feature of his emotional framework, or was it his mother Nina's relentless, alcohol-fueled infusions of self-doubt?

Mewshaw says: "I think it's important that we separate parents and family experiences from Jimmie Trimble. With regard to his family, yes, he felt alienated at an early age; he steeled himself early against future hurts. Concerning Trimble, I'm not sure that their relationship happened the way Vidal says it did. Certainly, they seem to have had an adolescent fixation with each other, a crush. I think that he used the Trimble story to great romantic fact almost like his fiction." Vidal himself wavered. In *Palimpsest*, Trimble figured in as a love match because "there wasn't any other." In *Point to Point Navigation*, Vidal replaces him with Austen.

Although close with school chum Trimble, Vidal didn't view writers as one big fraternity. Mewshaw excels at documenting both cutting and hilarious stories from their years together. His pages include Austen, with whom he claimed not to have sex with for decades; the ubiquitous Mickey Knox ("You have any idea how hard it is to get Burt Lancaster blown every night of the week?"); and various film stars, literati and glitterati – enough modern-day "selfies" to fill fleets of limousines.

Some of Vidal's guests were writers, not exactly his favorite group. "Writers are the only people who are reviewed by people of their own kind," Vidal said in an interview. "And their own kind can often be reasonably generous – *if* you stay in your category. I don't. I do many different things rather better than most people do one thing. And envy is the central fact of

American life." Wondering what kind of reception his writer friend John Berendt (*Midnight in the Garden of Good and Evil*) might receive, Sean Strub was worried as they made their way to Vidal's renowned Italian Villa La Rondinaia, off the Amalfi Coast. Strub remembers in *Body Counts: A Memoir of Politics, Sex, AIDS and Survival* his host's marathon drinking and moist eyes as he pined for actor Dick York. Despite his emotional armor, Vidal was a man capable of feeling, unlike his well-rehearsed trope: "I'm exactly as I appear. There is no warm, lovable person inside. Beneath my cold exterior, once you break the ice, you find cold water." Vidal's self-effacing description may have prompted Italo Calvino, whose work Vidal had introduced to U.S. readers in a *New York Review of Books* essay, to comment that he thought Vidal "had no unconscious."

Vidal's constant sex romps with hustlers, which Mewshaw describes so that readers can understand the man beneath the sex, comes up against Tim Teeman's *In Bed with Gore Vidal: Hustlers, Hollywood, and the Private World of an American Master*. Arch-conservative William F. Buckley, with whom Vidal sparred regularly in the era of early talk television, figures into things in a lurid way. Teeman asked Vidal's half-sister Nina Straight, "(Was) Vidal right to be afraid of Buckley, did she know the details of what Buckley held on Vidal(?)" She told him: "I can guess what they are. Jerry Sandusky acts." According to Teeman, Buckley claimed to hold evidence that Vidal was having sex with underage males. Upon asking, Straight nodded to him, "It would be hypothetical, but you can cover that range, yes." Teeman next asked if he would "be wrong to take from this that she is suggesting Vidal thought Buckley had incriminating evidence Vidal had sex with underage men.""No, you would not be incorrect in taking that from what I've said," replied Straight. When Teeman subsequently asked for further detail from Straight, she declined to comment.

Vidal does say in *Palimpsest* that he was "attracted to adolescent males." In a particularly riveting section of Teeman's book, Hollywood actor and director Burr Steers, Nina Straight's son, told him: "I know Buckley had a file on him that Gore feared. 'The file,' as he called it, was something he was afraid of. Buckley definitely had something over him. It would make sense if that material were about him having underage sex. Gore spent a lot of time in Bangkok, after all. My mother's younger brother (and Jacqueline Kennedy's half-brother) Jamie Auchincloss was caught with child pornography and was sent to jail, and Gore would not condemn him. (Auchincloss was indeed jailed in 2011 on such charges.) Gore also had a very weird take on the abuse perpetrated by Catholic priests – he would say that the young guys involved were hustlers who were sending signals. Gore was so twisted up about sex, there was a big difference between the public image he crafted and what he was about in reality." Does Steers know if his uncle had sex with underage men? "I don't know for sure and I don't want to know. But look, the love of his life was Jimmie Trimble, stuck forever as a teenage boy, a Peter Pan. The photo he carried around of Howard in his wallet wasn't of Howard as an adult, but Howard as a teenager." Vidal left his entire $37 million estate to Harvard University, but Straight and Steers are contesting the will, claiming he was not mentally competent when he filed it.

In 2012, according to the U.K.'s *Daily Mail*, Buckley's son Christopher wrote in an essay for *New Republic* that he had disposed of a file his father kept on Vidal. "When WFB (William F. Buckley) died, in 2008, I found in his study, more cluttered than King Tut's tomb, a file cabinet bursting to the seams, labeled 'Vidal Legal,'" Christopher wrote. "Into the dumpster it went, and I still remember the sigh of relief upon heaving it in." Mewshaw is clear that with regard to the unconfirmed Buckley story, he saw nothing askew. He says, "My wife and I raised our two boys around him. I saw no evidence that he took an unusual interest in them at an early age or even as teenagers. He liked rough trade. That was his thing." Perhaps Vidal's penchant for afternoon sex with hustlers had its origins in his father Eugene's heart attack, which did not kill him in middle age but prompted Vidal to advise: "The trick is to arrange for sex in the afternoon and save the booze and food for afterward."

Rough trade is perhaps what embroiled Edmund White in a legal scuffle with Vidal when he published *Terre Haute*, a play with characters based on an imagined series of conversations between Oklahoma City bomber Timothy McVeigh and Vidal. Perhaps there was a reason Vidal said, "Litigation takes the place of sex at middle age." Around that time, Mewshaw writes that Vidal was in one of his frequent "wanting to die" moods. Hoping to cajole him out of his funk, he told Vidal: "I like you. I don't want you to die." He closed this scene with the conclusion that Vidal "couldn't be jollied out of his bleak mood." He replied,

"Maybe you don't want me out of the way. But Edmund White, I bet he'd like to see me gone."

Regarding White, the biographer says, "I have no real detail on the Edmund White suit or threat of a suit. Vidal was a litigious man. That created the opportunity for many unfortunate incidents." He did remember that White at one point "explained to Vidal what he had intended with the play." Vidal nonetheless told *The Observer*: "Edmund White will yet be feeling the wrath of my lawyers. It's unethical and vicious to make it very clear that this old faggot writer is based on me, and that I'm madly in love with Timothy McVeigh, who I never met. (I don't want to be) lumped together with Mailer and Capote. They both went for murderers, and I don't go for murderers."

At the time, White told *The Telegraph* about the play's origins: "I thought, 'How can I do that? I can't imagine writing lines from McVeigh's point of view.' Then I remembered Gore Vidal had been in correspondence with him. I thought: 'Well, they never met, but wouldn't it be interesting if you changed the names and let them meet?' I've known Gore. We're roughly the same age group, we're both Europeanized Americans, we're both gay. I was presumptuous enough to write things from his point of view but as I went on writing the play, it became much more about me. Gore later told me: 'I would never have been attracted to someone like that.' But I would have been." White told the *New York Post's Page Six* that Vidal signed off on the portrayal: "I still have the fax saying it was OK by him. Maybe he forgot it, since he went into surgery the very next day. I

157

changed the names of the characters. I invented all the dialogue and actions, (and) the character of James ended up being closer to my experience and politics than to Mr. Vidal's. White also insists that nobody who reviewed the show made the mistake of confounding the character James with Gore Vidal. I hope upon reflection Mr. Vidal will withdraw his intention to sue me for libel."

"He never sued me, just threatened, but he had already given me his approval by fax," White confirmed in an email. "I wrote him a nice letter reminding him we'd first met in the 70s through Peggy Guggenheim," he added, at her Venice residence where she entertained the world's A-list. "I asked him for a blurb for *Nocturnes for the King of Naples*, which he gave me." It reads: "A baroque invention of quite startling brilliance and intensity."

Mewshaw concludes about Vidal: "Even though he died with $37 million amassed, he always had a deep sense of disappointment that he had not gone through his entire list of what you hope to achieve, being elected a Senator, even President. Of course, he would never have been elected to public office in the years that he ran because there were too many behind the scene negatives that opponents would force to be exposed." For example, he points out that Vidal sought "Irish citizenship as a way to avoid paying taxes. He spent many years living in Italy saying publicly he needed to leave the United States in order to see it more clearly and coincidentally he had maneuvered lucrative tax breaks that made it all possible. So he was, in a sense, both noble and practical."

Perhaps one of the master's own quotes offers a glimpse of what is yet to come of his legacy: "The greatest pleasure when I started making money was not buying cars or yachts but finding myself able to have as many freshly typed drafts as possible." With as rich a life as he lived, there are many drafts still to come on the life of Gore Vidal.

EIGHTEEN WRITERS DIGEST CHRISTOPHER ISHERWOOD'S 1939 MIGRATION TO THE US

In *The American Isherwood* edited by James J. Berg (born 1964) and Chris Freeman (born 1965), eighteen writers in essay form cover Christopher Isherwood's 1939 migration to the US, *A Single Man period*, his spiritual life and relationship to Swami Prabhavananda, Isherwood's friends, Hollywood's celebrity culture, and the reception of gay-themed writing in 1960s Cold War America – revealing how Isherwood used autobiographical experience in his writing as a lens to focus on the world and his times.

Readers will discover that although Isherwood 's heritage stretches back to the early 20th century, his experiences and the themes covered by the slate of writers reflecting on his work remain remarkably relevant to today's civil rights issues and political upheavals worldwide.

The most interesting tidbit for me was discovering that Isherwood never saw Cabaret on the Broadway stage during its three-year run from 1966 to 1969. His 1939 novel *Goodbye to Berlin* was the basis for the musical Cabaret. Isherwood traveled to Berlin in 1929 to experience its gay scene.

Reviewing this book prompted a few surprises! An old friend from my home area and later a NYC denizen of Studio 54 and other amusements, Helen Irwin, edited the manuscript for Berg and Freeman. They all kept residences in Palm Springs. In the mid-1970s, she became Managing Editor of Bob Guccione's avant-garde women's magazine, *Viva*, where she hired Anna Wintour for her first job in the US in 1976. During those years, Helen was inspired by her friend Michael Parish to get a share on Fire Island. Photographer Tom Bianchi, one of her housemates, documented those years in his book, *Fire Island* and he talks about Helen in the introduction. The literary and disco-infused weekends gave her all the latest New York gossip, which helped her keep *Viva* in the know. Helen published a memoir in GLR in the summer of 2015 called *Who Was That Woman in the Pines?*

The basic tenet of the artfully edited *The American Isherwood* by James J. Berg and Chris Freeman (University of Minnesota Press) is that a writer owns nothing else but his experience. In this sense, Christopher Isherwood was an "existentialist," not in a murky hopeless way but by firmly clutching the idea that experience counts as primary in our lives. "Because, after all, what else does he really have?" he asked about writers. The collected essays begin with Isherwood's migration to the US in 1939.

"What I know is what I am," Christopher Isherwood said. What he knew by the time he died in 1986 as a cis, white, gay man remains startlingly relevant to the current ultra-diverse queer universe. A "camera with its shutter open" is the most frequently used metaphor describing Isherwood's work. Readers with shutters open will see parallels with the iconic writer's struggles and today's issue-making headlines.

The editors do a marvelous job of organizing the book into three sections and beginning each section with a piece that provides context for the essays that follow. The first section is devoted to Isherwood's *A Single Man*. The second section considers the author's well-known spiritual life and relationship to guru swami Prabhavananda. The third section focuses on Isherwood's work as it relates to friends, Hollywood's celebrity culture, and the reception of gay-themed writing in 1960s Cold War America. Richly detailed gems culled from Isherwood's archive provide Berg and Freeman's introductory pieces and the essayists' portrayals with deep authenticity. Although at moments turgidly academic, the essays are accessible to general readers.

The book's first section is a comprehensive look at *A Single Man* and its relationship to E.M. Forster's *Maurice* and Virginia Woolf's *Mrs. Dalloway*.

Following a visit with Edward Carpenter, Forster began writing *Maurice* resolving that he would not let his story end tragically. The 81-year-old Forster subsequently explained: "a happy ending was imperative. I was determined that in fiction anyway two men should fall in love and remain in it for the ever and ever that fiction allows." Like Isherwood's fiction challenged, Woolf's Clarissa Dalloway and "shell-shocked" soldier Septimus Smith explored "normative" mourning. She wanted her characters "to criticize the social system" in much the same way Jasbir Puar's concept of "homonationalism" (*Terrorist Assemblages: Homonationalism in Queer Times*, Duke University Press) shreds current belief systems around equality if defined primarily by marriage and military service, the happy endings Isherwood and Woolf's characters were denied.

Threads lacing through the essays bring to mind that homosexuals are raised in a patriarchal society. Since many gay men now openly mature against a backdrop of post-Don't Ask, Don't Tell and court-supported same-sex marriage, are they filling the ranks of a new patriarchy? How is military service and marriage for gay men (and lesbians, bisexual, and transgender people) different from the old patriarchy that denied Isherwood's George and Woolf's Smith the satisfactions of open relationships? In Jamie Carr's essay *Writing the Unspeakable in A Single Man and Mrs. Dalloway*, she quotes Erin Carlston's *Thinking Fascism: Sapphic Modernism and Fascist Modernity*: "...to be disloyal to patriarchy – by flouting the paradigms of compulsory heterosexuality...is to be disloyal to the patria, to call into question the terms of one's membership in the national community."

For example, now that queer men and women are allowed to serve openly in the Armed Forces will they feel comfortable challenging military policies? Or will they acquiesce, fearing the tarnishment by the old myth that queers (Isherwood's preferred term) are a new kind of security risk? Thus, forming a new patriarchy. That's Puar's point regarding homonationalism: How LGBT "acceptance" and "tolerance" have become the barometer by which the right to and capacity for national sovereignty is evaluated.

In 2011, Sarah Schulman wrote in the *New York Times* about "the co-opting of white gay people by anti-immigrant and anti-Muslim political forces in Western Europe and Israel." Maya Mikdashi writes in *Jadaliyya* (Dec. 16, 2011): "A gay Israeli in a military uniform is both an enemy and a target of anti-occupation politics, just as a gay Zionist in the United States is an enemy of the Palestinian cause and the cause of queer Palestinians because they are rooted within that Palestinian national cause." In other words, does the kind of inclusion not socially acceptable in *Maurice* or *Mrs. Dalloway* but now allowed thwart resistance to military policies by LGBT soldiers because they fear a return to exclusion?

Perhaps *Out in the Dark* illustrates the tension between equal rights and political obligations to one's nation. The film centers on the love affair between two men on opposite sides of the Middle East conflict: Palestinian student Nimer and Roy, an Israeli lawyer. Deeply in love, Israeli security forces eventually force Nimer's deportation from Tel Aviv back to Ramallah, where he is immediately rounded up and killed by Palestinian militants for being a possible collaborator *and* for being gay. And even with full acceptance into the US military and marriage rights, Employment Non-Discrimination legislation (ENDA) has been introduced in every Congress since 1994 except the 109th. Similar legislation has been introduced without passage since 1974. Twenty-nine states do not have anti-discrimination statutes prohibiting discrimination and 38 do not have law prohibiting gender identity discrimination. Yet we can marry on Saturday, go to war Monday while a spouse reports to work and is fired for being gay. So, the question becomes, how does a recently married, newly minted queer soldier in the US, Israeli or Palestinian army react to such circumstances? By towing the same line as Woolf's Septimus Smith or Isherwood's George who shielded his grief from those around him?

Isherwood both wondered and worried about the life of his queer community. After the 1954 publication of *The World in the Evening*, he received stacks of fan mail. He said at one point about the letters: "...it's heart-breaking, the sense you get of all these island existences, dotted about like stars and nebulae" much like the *alienation nouveau* recently chronicled by a LOGO study – *Gay Men in America: Community at a Crossroads*–sampling 1,000 gay men ages 18-49.

Results reveal that while acceptance is at an all-time high, 61% of gay men in their 20s and 30s believe "in the past, the gay community was more united than it is today." Eighty-five percent agree "even as gay people become more accepted, we should have places that are just for us."

Six in 10 gay men in their 20s say "now that gay marriage is legal in so many places, my family expects me to get married and have children one day" and perhaps populate a new patriarchy? Even though 88% agree "gay people shouldn't have to conform to straight people's norms and values."

Sixty percent agree "it's harder for younger gay men to take advice from older gay men because the world is so different today." Perhaps not if your next book club includes Christopher Isherwood.

JAY PARINI DISCUSSES GORE VIDAL IN HIS OFFICIAL BIOGRAPHY

Jay Parini was born in 1948 – the same year Gore Vidal published *The City and the Pillar*, his book on U.S. homosexuality that blacklisted him with reviewers for many years thereafter. Sales chart busters published the same year included Norman Mailer's *The Naked and the Dead*, Truman Capote's *Other Voices, Other Rooms* and Alfred Kinsey's *Sexual Behavior in the Human Male*.

In *Empire of Self: A Life of Gore Vidal*, Parini discusses his relationship with the thin-skinned writer; William Buckley on the "pedophile" issue; and Jimmy Trimble, Vidal's first love. He also reflects on Tim Teeman's popular *In Bed with Gore Vidal*.

Parini and I grew up near each other in Pennsylvania's Anthracite Coal Region. There's more overlap. The 1948 Democratic National Convention chose sitting President Harry Truman as their candidate. My father serve as an elected Democratic delegate from his Congressional district. Vidal told Rolling Stone's Jan Wenner "In 1948, I wanted to go into politics," ensconcing himself in New Mexico where Governor Thomas J. Mabry was friendly with his grandfather Senator Thomas Gore. Mabry was to place Vidal on that year's ballot as a presidential elector, using Vidal's Hispanic sounding Austrian name and his state-level machine to bolster him. But alas,

Vidal ultimately decided to publish *City* making him a pariah among book reviewers. Vidal rejoined electoral politics with unsuccessful runs in 1960 for the U.S. House and U.S. Senate in 1982.

I wanted to hear from Parini about the practicalities and turmoil that can accompany serving as a bold-face author's official biographer.

What is the correct lineage of Vidal's biographers?
Vidal had selected Walter Clemons, who, unfortunately, suffered from diabetes and frequent writer's block and had died before any chance of completing the project. Gore begged me to take it on: "Please, please be my official biographer."

My wife warned me against doing so fearing we would never be friends again. Gore was very thin-skinned and could not tolerate even the slightest criticism. I declined but began writing notes for a book that could only be published after Vidal's death. Then I ran into Fred Kaplan at a writer's conference, and I asked him to do me a favor and take on Gore's biography, which I may have suggested to him earlier but cannot remember for sure. He agreed (*Gore Vidal: A Biography*, 1999) but the problem is that Gore hated the book and, in my presence, threw it across the room. Kaplan focused on Gore's youth and a lot on his money issues early in his adult life. Reviewers were also rough, arguing the 800 pages had no 'through line' or central argument. After that, I came into the picture as Gore's official biographer.

When writing about a famous author who acknowledges how easy it is to misremember one's life, how did you guard against misremembering Vidal's life?

I was constantly making notes. And biography is 80% agreed-upon fact and 20% interpretation. As his official biographer, I had full access to his archives, letters, notes, and interviews with many who knew him. I also have about 25 years' worth of notes, clippings, and notebooks on him.

His literary estate helped with setting up interviews, provided access to his diary entries. I had access to anything I thought I needed.

At the end of each chapter, you include your own experiences with Vidal. They were intimate moments...

Yes, they were very close moments for us. Visiting Rock Creek, where he lived when his mother married Hugh Auchincloss, or peeking into the windows of Edgewater, the first home he purchased in upstate New York. It was a last-minute thought to feed the stories. I must have at least 100 or more of them. I thought it would be a good way to declare my interest in the subject.

Jimmy Trimble – a real or imagined affair?

Imagined but something he certainly got a lot of mileage out of over the years. He was an adolescent who knows about adolescent crushes. A school chum, Barrett Prettyman, swore the relationship never happened. I think it was all Gore's perception and that Trimble would have been shocked to know how Gore felt about him, real or imagined.

As a schoolboy, was Vidal a classic underachiever?
He was deeply stunted emotionally over the problems he had with his mother, especially her rampant alcoholism. It had always been a very rough relationship between them. That is what led to his being shuffled off to his grandparents, one of whom was, of course, Senator Gore. That is where, at about age 10, he began reading the congressional record to his grandfather who suffered from poor vision and was legally blind. Years later when visiting Gore at home I could see that he was obsessive about his research for his historical novels. Even as we sat there talking with one another he had stacks of history books that he would pour through for details.

The movie Best of Enemies, *about 1968 and Vidal's cantankerous relationship with William F. Buckley Jr, shows them baring teeth but did they actually need one another? At one point, Vidal whispers into Buckley's ear, "I guess we gave them their money's worth tonight?"*
They were both actors. They knew what they were doing. I had dinner with Gore and Norman Mailer, another of his newsworthy relationships. All three of them were true to their beliefs and actions.

Speaking of famous relationships, Vidal always peddled that he was an "intimate" of the Kennedys. You disagree.
He was more of an "onlooker" than an insider. They were not in each other's company that many times. Now, remember, he

and Jackie shared a stepfather when each of their respective mothers married Hugh Auchincloss. But that was before she was a Kennedy.

Vidal's half-sister, Nina Straight, and her son Burr Steers, while talking to Tim Teeman, author of In Bed with Gore Vidal, *brought up the "pedophile" issue regarding Vidal. William Buckley also intimated for years that he too thought Vidal was involved with underage males. Thoughts?*
That's just nuts, insane. He was not a pedophile. He really didn't like children although he was always polite to those children in his orbit. Did he have sex with younger men, 20 to 25 or even older when he was himself much older? Of course. He never hid that fact, at least not among his inner circles.

Why bring it up?
I think Nina thought she was going to get millions more than she got. Burr had been promised Gore's LA house and, somehow, that was reneged on in his will.

Vidal's lifelong partner Howard was always the mysterious one to those outside of the inner circle. What role did he play in his life?
I loved Howard. He was funny, a mensch. They truly loved one another but there were some rough times. In the '70s, Howard seriously thought about leaving Gore who had begun acting rudely toward him.

Howard could tell Vidal to shut up?

171

Yes, especially when Gore was full of himself, drunk, or both. Howard would say, "Okay, that's enough Gore" or "Time to shut up!" They were like any longtime married couple.

He had all kinds of moments?
He did. I've been at dinner parties where Gore was the delight of the evening, holding everyone in the palm of his hand, charming, funny as one could be. At other dinner parties he was plain drunk, slurry. As a friend, you'd be embarrassed for him. He was thin-skinned and could be dismissive of others. With me, and I know with others too, he was also kind, and solicitous. He always asked about my wife and children. We talked on the phone constantly. Once I arrived at his home and asked how he was doing. He said," Better now that you're here." Like all of us, he had a range of emotions.

He's part of you?
Gore was an important part of my life. This has been cathartic for me. Writing the book helped me to understand our friendship. We also write to get rid of stuff. Then, move on.

SUSAN QUINN UNRAVELS ELEANOR ROOSEVELT AND LORENA HICKOK'S LOVE AFFAIR

As a history buff, I was looking forward to reading and reviewing *Eleanor and Hick: The Love Affair That Shaped a First Lady*. Author Susan Quinn (born 1940) is a PEN New England Award recipient. Based on letters between Eleanor Roosevelt and *Associated Press* reporter Lorena Hickok (known as Hick), the book unravels their complicated relationship. Quinn's premise is in stark contrast to author Doris Faber's 1980 book, who was, Quinn says, "shocked" at the letters' content and left them out in her account of their relationship. Just like *Fox News* might do today with stories that don't fit their world view.

Quinn is nonjudgmental when correcting the public record. She wasn't championing any particular point of view; she just likes her history accurate, letting details fall where they may and allowing readers to decide. In 1948, The *New Yorker* magazine's E. J. Kahn wrote a much-read two-part profile of Eleanor, then 63, following FDR's death. "There's no getting around the fact that Eleanor Roosevelt is still the first lady of this country," a Democratic official said at the time. According to others, Kahn noted, "she can be even more aptly termed the first lady of the world." And Eleanor was happily in love with another woman at the time.

I've always had a hankering for the Roosevelts. They were kitchen table talk in my house. My father served in FDR's and (Harry Truman's) the Office of the Price Administration. I have unused gas rationing cards in my family archive. My brother Louis was born on April 12, 1942, three years before FDR died on the same day.

What won't die is the truth of Eleanor and Hick's relationship. Quinn reverses Napoleon Bonaparte's famous saying, "History is a set of lies agreed upon," his way of noting how history is manipulated and interpreted based on the prevailing narrative. Although the narrative has changed, many among us are fixated on a "love that dare not speak its name" as wrote Lord Alfred Douglas in his poem *Two Loves*. The phrase was used against Oscar Wilde in his 1895 trial on charges of gross indecency, a United Kingdom law often used against queers.

~ ~

"It was a deep and loving relationship."
We like our history in a straight line. Yet, time and again it twists and turns to deliberately throw us off.

Sue Quinn's remarkable new book *Eleanor and Hick: The Love Affair That Shaped a First Lady* helps readers unravel the complicated, but loving, relationship between Eleanor Roosevelt, wife of Franklin Delano Roosevelt, and *Associated Press* reporter Lorena Hickok, known as a lesbian during her professional years.

Quinn's account is based on the letters between Eleanor and Hick, as she was known, released 40 years ago – 10 years after her death, as called for by Eleanor's estate. Hickok covered Eleanor during the last months of FDR's 1932 presidential campaign, when, according to Doris Kearns Goodwin in *No Ordinary Time: Franklin and Eleanor Roosevelt: The Home Front in World War II*, she "fell madly in love with her." At the 1933 inauguration, Eleanor wore a sapphire ring Hickok had given her.

Herein is the significance of Quinn's contribution to the Roosevelt canon: She ably dismantles the first book written after release of the sumptuous letters.

In 1980 author Doris Faber, who was, Quinn says, "shocked" at the letters' content in her account of their relationship in *The Life of Lorena Hickok: E.R.'s Friend*. Faber denies any sexual dimension between the women. In fact, when their letters were released in 1977 and Faber began her manuscript work, she begged librarians to seal them back up. That two women – a first lady – might have a passionate relationship was just too much for her. Researcher Leila J. Rupp criticized Faber's argument, calling her book "a case study in homophobia" and arguing that Faber unwittingly presented "page after page of evidence that delineates the growth and development of a love affair between the two women."

"Attitudes change. I re-examined their relationship. After all, they gave each other satisfaction and joy," Quinn said.

Hickok encouraged Eleanor to hold her own press conferences for women journalists. To turn her daily letters to her into Eleanor's famous "My Day" newspaper column. "Hick helped Eleanor find her voice," Quinn explained.

When their relationship flourished, many female activists in the Democratic Party of the 1930s were lesbian. "Women who loved women were all around Eleanor," Quinn says.

And Eleanor did have her challenging sorrows.

Hired in 1914, her social secretary Lucy Mercer and FDR kindled a relationship thought to have first sparked in 1916. In 1918, Franklin traveled to Europe to inspect naval facilities for World War I. He returned sick with pneumonia in both lungs. That's when Eleanor discovered a packet of love letters from Mercer in his suitcase. She offered him a divorce which he refused. FDR's mother, Sara Delano Roosevelt, was adamantly against their divorcing, sure it would end his political career. She threatened to cut him off from the family fortune if he chose to do so.

Goodwin summarized their letters thus: "Hick longed to kiss the soft spot at the corner of Eleanor's mouth; Eleanor yearned to hold Hick close; Hick despaired at being away from Eleanor; and Eleanor wished she could lie down beside Hick and take her in her arms. Day after day, month after month, the tone in the letters on both sides remains fervent and loving." She concluded, however, that "whether Hick and Eleanor went beyond kisses and hugs" cannot be known for certain, and that the important issue is the impact the close relationship had on both women's lives. In contrast, a 2011 essay by Russell Baker reviewing two new Roosevelt biographies in the *New York Times Review of Books* stated, "That the Hickok relationship was indeed erotic now seems beyond dispute considering what is known about the letters they exchanged."

Eleanor also had a known relationship with FDR's bodyguard, Earl Miller. They swam together, went horseback riding and had long drives. No one knows for sure if they were sexual.

"The relationship between Eleanor and Hick was very important to both of them," Quinn says. "It was a deep and loving relationship."

Readers can decide for themselves how to label Eleanor and Hick's love for each other. History is not a straight line.

WHAT DO YOU THINK ABOUT WHEN YOU THINK OF EQUALITY? BY PAUL ALAN FAHEY

In *Equality: What Do You Think About When You Think of Equality?* by Paul Alan Fahey (1944-2017), readers are treated to 25 essays by assorted writers interrogating the meaning of equality – some based on a single experience, others weaving several personal events into a pattern, all transformative. Fahey died September 12, 2017.

The essays are thought-provoking and offered in the same tradition as *Stride Toward Freedom* by Dr. Martin Luther King and *I Am Malala* by Malala Yousafzai. With book banning all the rage in some circles, I could not specifically find Fahey's title on any banned list, a list I'm tangentially connected to as a result of New College of Florida's 2024 ban of *When I Knew* by fashion and celebrity photographer Robert Trachtenberg published in 2005. In 2008, award-winning filmmakers Fenton Bailey and Randy Barbato recreated their version of the book's premise with fresh interviews in a film by the same name. I sat for two segment tapings but was not selected for the final cut. Instead, the filmmakers used a photograph of me at the age of five on the DVD cover. I guess that makes it an 'out of town' banning?

Like Fahey, and apparently Bailey and Barbato, I like to

listen to others' whys and wherefores on life and its challenges. And certainly since Fahey's book was released nearly a decade ago, discussions of 'equality' have focused on, as Bill Maher has noted in my interviews with him about Conservatives and politically-aligned Christians: "Their right to take away your right." And since the heady years of Stonewall-energized political and legislative actions by queers at all levels across the nation, much of what was fought for is now in retrenchment under a solid backlash of heightened hate and violence toward the queer community.

~~~

*Is equality like obscenity? * You'll know it when you see it?*
Readers may get the same impression when reading *Equality: What Do You Think About When You Think of Equality?* Compiled and edited by now deceased Paul Alan Fahey, this collection of 25 essays by assorted writers interrogates the meaning of equality. For some essayists, conclusions are based on a single experience, while others weave several personal events into a pattern; all are transformative readings.

In *Give Us Our Birthright*, on reviving the Equal Rights Amendment, Susan Reynolds underscores the importance of knowing social justice history, summarizing the ERA's lineage from the 1848 Women's Rights Conference with Elizabeth Cady Stanton to Alice Paul and Crystal Eastman, who penned the ERA and introduced it to Congress in 1923. Still alive in 1972 when the last iteration of an ERA measure was passed by

Congress for states' consideration, Alice Paul inspired the new era's Women's Movement—Gloria Steinem, Bella Abzug, New York Congresswoman Shirley Chisholm (I heard Chisholm deliver her 1972 Presidential campaign speech, the most inspiring speech I've ever heard). Chisholm was the first woman and the first African-American person to seek the Democratic Party's presidential nomination.

In his remembrance of Lani Silver, writer David Congalton addresses the pace of social change. Silver told Congalton, "We've gone from Jasper to an African-American president…in a single decade," referring to the hot June night in Jasper, Texas, in 1998, when James Byrd, Jr. was beaten and tied by his ankles to the back of a truck by three men offering him a ride. With his head severed after a 3.5 mile dragging, police found body parts in 84 different places along the road.

Like Nathan Manske's brilliant LGBT-themed video project, *I'm from Driftwood*, Silver always spoke directly to those oppressed. Humbly, that's good advice for us all to follow. She talked to 2,600 people in Jaspers, Houston, and San Francisco asking them: How has racism affected your life?

Listening to others rather than simply talking allows for understanding nuance and explaining history. Listening to himself is how Fahey concocted the idea for his book. "After Proposition 8 was declared unconstitutional, I realized I could marry Robert after being together 37 years. Now I know what equality means," he thought at that moment. The contributor's list is intersectional by design. "I made up my dream list of writers and they all came through," Fahey writes.

Writer Christopher Bram notes that Thomas Jefferson's 1776 Declaration of Independence mentions equality only once. That nice abstract phrase becomes important only when equality becomes reality in the form of successive movements beyond white, land-owning, slave-owning men—emancipation, women's suffrage, civil rights, gay rights, et cetera.

In *Everyday Equality*, Barbara Jacksha offers a challenging thought: true equality demands no conformity and embraces all sexual preferences. Her essay walks readers through asking if she treats others the way she hopes to be treated. Jacksha's piece dovetails nicely with Catherine Ryan Hyde's essay, "When I Think of Equality," in which Hyde pokes at us with her challenge to imagine a world in which "we all applied our beliefs to our own lives and left everybody else the hell alone."

Searching his soul, the author Nathan Burgoine reflects that "life as a queer is halfway, and halfway, and halfway," a conclusion he reached after discussing marriage with a long-time straight friend. His easygoing style reflects a lovable feature of Fahey's collection: it's not tight-as-a-frog's-ass academic. Essayists aren't defending their doctoral theses against arcane counterpoints. They're simply remembering experiences. All in all, a refreshing political read for today's modern reader.

*In the obscenity case of *Jacobellis v. Ohio* (1964), US

181

Supreme Court Justice Potter Stewart wrote that "hard-core pornography" was hard to define, but "I know it when I see it."

MARTIN DUBERMAN'S *JEWS, QUEERS, GERMANS: A NOVEL*

Martin Duberman, historian, biographer, playwright, and gay rights activist, has written more than 25 books. In *Jews, Queers, Germans: A Novel*, he offers a gripping account of documented history in novel form. Readers eavesdrop on Kaiser Wilhelm, Fritz Krupp, Count Harry Kessler, Walter Rathenau, and Prince Philipp of Eulenburg.

Regarding the vailed man-on-man themes reflected in his novel's depictions, Duberman quoted the London Gay Liberation Manifesto in his book *Has the Gay Movement Failed?* (2018). He stressed that "The ultimate success of all forms of oppression is our self-oppression. Self-oppression is achieved when the gay person has adopted and internalized straight people's definition of what is good and bad."

His perspectives on national politics was ahead of the anointed ongoing narrative. Duberman issued his warning in this historical novel: Donald Trump and Kaiser Wilhelm "represent petulant boys, spoiled bullies." He's said more recently in interviews that he hopes "Trump will see some of his trials begin in 2024." So much that moment of optimism.

Upon publication, Duberman emailed to say that he appreciated my treatment of his work "and for writing about it at such length."

Without history there is no freedom. And the history that Martin Duberman masterfully unravels in *Jews, Queers, Germans: A Novel* is remarkable for the territory covered.

He calls the book a novel/history, a clever mixture of documented history in novel form that is a gripping read. "I never invent anything that is contrary to the known record," Duberman told *Windy City Times*. "I had a lot of angst writing this book, thinking about how it might be received by traditional historians."

The book opens with Margarethe, wife of Fritz Krupp, who made all of Germany's armaments during World War I and therefore vital to Germany's interests as Europe unravels. She informs Kaiser Wilhelm II that her husband's affairs with comely teenage boys is moving from whispers to headlines. Eventually, there's a salacious trial, much like the 1895 Oscar Wilde case.

"I started with Magnus Hirschfeld but the more I got into the period the more I became intrigued with several others," Duberman explained. To tell the entire story, Duberman convenes Count Harry Kessler, Walter Rathenau, and Prince Philipp of Eulenburg.

Regarding Kaiser Wilhelm, "there has never been consensus that he was gay. There has been reporting on contemporary speculation about his relationships," Duberman says in the book. Kaiser Wilhelm was a member of the infamous Eulenburg group and consequently became embroiled in the Eulenburg Affair, the biggest domestic affair between the formation of the Reich in 1871 and the abdication of Kaiser Wilhelm II in 1918. Prince Philipp, whom Wilhelm called "my bosom friend ... the only one I have," was accused of homosexuality and almost immediately fell in disgrace and lost all his influence on German policy.

I've always been interested in my historical characters' feelings, relationships, and fantasies, their whole psychology. I've always been intrigued with the story part of the story. And what grabs me I write about," Duberman writes. "And I do think that for the people I'm writing about there is a lot of camp. The tone of irony has long been part of the gay subculture." The pages are lush with descriptions of internecine love affairs, tailors who craft military uniforms with exquisite gaydar. Testimony during Krupp's trial by a soldier about his wearing white tights and black boots makes a reader's eyes roll.

The historical characters Duberman selected were precursors to today's dialogues.

Hirschfeld, founder of the Scientific Humanitarian Committee, thought he could identify homosexuals by their distinguishing effeminate qualities. Although that's true for some guys (and so what) that's not true of all (and not all effeminate guys are gay). And that's the point: No maxim about human sexuality or behavior is universal.

In opposition to Hirschfeld, The Community of the Special butched it up by promoting the masculine, Greek ideal. Perhaps they were extraordinarily insecure about who they loved. Men of all sexualities overcompensate for many reasons.

Next came The League of Human Rights, a home for Conservative homosexuals like our current CPAC, the Conservative Political Action Conference. Some CPAC members today (as were League some members?) are transgender. Transgender Conservative activists Jennifer Williams and Jordan Evans caused a stir when last February they attended CPAC. The annual event has been home to Ronald Reagan, Sarah Palin, and President Donald Trump. CPAC's website hails itself as the "birthplace of modern conservatism" and the conference as an "Activism Boot Camp." Williams said in a recent interview she became a conservative "because of Jimmy Carter and the Iran hostage crisis."

Also in a recent interview, Gina Roberts, chair of the San Diego Log Cabin Republicans, a chapter of the nation's largest gay GOP political organization said, "I believe Conservative principles are more closely aligned with the intent of the U.S. Constitution. Conservatism leads to smaller, less invasive government."

It is remarkable how much we have changed and how much we have remained the same. Arguments made 100 years ago about the nature of human sexuality – and homosexuality – continue today.

"People have not changed in the 100 years since all of this has taken place. The political environments in which they operate have changed but not the people," Duberman observes. For example, Kaiser Wilhelm had many unappealing qualities: "his adolescent humor, his harshness, his inability to listen; his pretension to knowledge and wisdom he doesn't possess; his assumption of infallibility in all matters…his limited attention span…"

Trump?

"Well, I started writing the book in 2015 much before the Trump phenomena. And it turns out there's lots that resonates with a person like President Trump. He and Wilhelm represent petulant boys, spoiled bullies," Duberman writes.

One chilling coincidence is when in 1923 Hitler tried to take over Germany's Ruhr district using the slogan Make Germany Great Again. His efforts were fueled by German perceptions that the nation was being disgraced by the conditions of the Versailles Treaty. The political scenario sounds alarmingly like Trump's claims that our trade agreements and treaties make chumps of the United States. And he alone can fix the problem.

Paragraph 175, the section of the German legal code which criminalized homosexuality, figures into the story. The infamous section of law resembles today's anti-transgender "bathroom bills" aimed at making self-expression illegal. Opposing propaganda machines worked hard to make linkages. "Groups tried to link Nazis to homosexuals, Jews to homosexuals," Duberman explains. Attempts to link opponents to homosexuals resembles the current "gay conspiracy" theories about the gay community's plan to take over, well, everything. Interestingly enough, during the years before Joseph Stalin took over from Vladimir Lenin, Russia had begun the process of decriminalizing homosexuality. Today in Chechnya there are horrible reports of homosexuals being rounded up, beaten, killed.

The old guilt by association trick used decades later by the US House Un-American Committee (HUAC) against State Department officials makes appearances in the book.

Then, like now, who is and who isn't "homosexual" – and what that means still fuels debate. Maybe RuPaul said it best when he told *The New Yorker* – "we're born naked and the rest is drag".

Duberman said in a previous interview "As I get older, I get still more radical" And he confirms that "Yes that's still true. Strange but true."

He may be getting more radical but he has not slowed down. He invited me to attend two panels he assembled on April 22, 2017 to discuss Beyond Marriage and Beyond Equality with leading fellow scholars and activists. They held forth with provocative discussions that examined LGBT political advancements at the time – and the cultural price paid for assimilation. Duberman anticipates writing a book asking the question *Has the Gay Movement Failed?* but not before releasing *The Rest of It*, the third and final memoir. "I've chronicled my whole life and now here's the rest of it," he said.

For readers who want to revisit Duberman or are virgins, there is *The Martin Duberman Reader*, a compilation of his most important writings that gives readers an overview of our times. His essays provide a new generation of activists, scholars, and readers benchmark understandings of what has come before us. For five decades, Duberman has tackled the complex and the inconvenient and produced definitive biographies (Paul Robeson, Lincoln Kirstein, and Howard Zinn), essays, books, plays, reviews, and commentary. He founded the nation's first graduate program in LGBT studies and is well known for his book on the Stonewall riots, a set of close-up portraits of six participants of the event that gave birth to the modern gay movement.

LESBIAN AVENGER CO-FOUNDER ANNE-CHRISTINE D'ADESKY ON ACT UP AND HER MEMOIR

My review and interview with Anne-christine d'Adesky about *The Pox Lover: An Activist's Decade in New York and Paris* covers her years of living and working in both cities in the 1990s. Her rich memories delineate the non-stop work as a pioneering AIDS and queer journalist and as co-founder of The Lesbian Avengers.

d'Adesky discusses 1990s radical lesbian activism, often overshadowed by the work of gay men during that era, and the pitfalls of LGBTQ assimilation. Her work today would be called "intersectional." She was *Out* senior editor, founded *HIV Plus*, and has written for the *Advocate*, the *Village Voice*, the *San Francisco Examiner*, and the *New York Native*.

Days before publishing her interview, we gathered at the LGBT Community Center in Manhattan's Greenwich Village where d'Adesky co-hosted *The Bodies on the Line*, celebrating living and deceased editors and reporters who chronicled the HIV epidemic. An HIV Reporting Scholarship, named The Kiki, after Curtis "Kiki" Mason, was launched. We both wrote for *POZ* magazine and were from Pennsylvania, we both faced a deadly diagnosis of Kaposi's sarcoma. My doctor describing my condition as the worst case she'd ever seen. Kiki successfully advocated for a successful chemotherapy agent that he did not survive long enough to use himself. He died just months before its release; I benefitted from the trial I after learning of it from him. He was honored on the 30th anniversary of ACT UP.

The scholarship is awarded to a reporter focused on HIV coverage and is administered by NLGJA – The Association of LGBTQ Journalists. "Many of these journalists were extraordinary. "They pioneered how they were going to cover it, and often they themselves were struggling with or dying of AIDS," according to *POZ Magazine*.

$$\sim\!\!\text{\tiny m}$$

Gore Vidal remarked that each time we remember something we are remembering the last time we thought of the event. Our memory has multiple layers, a palimpsest.
The book was a way of going back through my diaries. Thinking back to those days and the words I had written then. Trying to understand what happened then and present it to readers now. Doing so I also wanted to continue the conversations that we all had then. I'm hoping readers will think about where they were as I chart my way through my own life events. Readers' moments in time are as important as mine.

What sparked the founding, with others, of the Lesbian Avengers?
The first feeling we had was that as lesbians we were invisible to the public. We had issues—health, political, economic—that we dealt with but were not part of the public dialogue. Yet we had

done so much in solidarity with other groups around women's health. We'd been vital parts of The Feminist Movement, ACT UP, peace movements. The time came for us to advocate for ourselves. But we also wanted to have some fun. We wanted to poke fun at the old stereotypes of lesbian separatism. Poke fun at the angry lesbian. We intentionally chose the D word, dyke. All of our public activity was a way of empowering ourselves. We had so much experience at movement organizing and politics that we began applying what we learned to ourselves. Why sleep? There was so much work to do.

Humor helped you survive the 90s? Dancing, too?
Oh absolutely. The Avengers would do things like create a huge bed and go down New York City's Fifth Avenue. With lesbians romping all over the bed. We wanted intentionally to be cheeky and have fun. We had learned so much from the ACT UP visuals that later helped us to show lesbian sexuality in a public way. And I still go dancing all night long!

When protease inhibitors for the treatment of HIV became available in late 1995, early 1996, was that a turning point?
We called it the Lazarus Effect: people rose up from their sick beds, able to begin healing now that the combination of three HIV medicines could successfully attack the virus and reverse its effects. Before that time, AIDS was a death sentence. I remember my dear friend Kiki Mason in the book. He wrote a regular column called "Life" for *POZ* magazine in the early days, 1994 forward, on his deteriorating condition. Once he wrote "I'm not dying; I'm being murdered. I am being sold down the

river by people within this community who claim to be helping people with AIDS." Kiki was intense in his ways and that's what makes him unforgettable.

In interviews John Waters has said, "What's wrong with these kids today? Not getting married and not serving in the Army are what made being gay so much fun!" What's your take on assimilation-versus-outlaw?

Nothing wrong with assimilation, but it leaves behind the rest of us who maybe don't want to be like everyone else. The fight isn't over. Critical issues remain that the LGBT community must address—race, class, religion—within our own ranks and in the larger community. These issues affect all of us negatively, queer and non-queer, alike.

Although she did not win France's last presidential election, Marine Le Pen, daughter of Jean-Marie Le Pen, founder of France's far-right wing Front National party, raised hackles because of her gay male supporters.

Privileged, gay men in France crafted a very effective image for her. It is a failure of the French left to not have attracted more of the gay community into its ranks. As I said in a recent *Advocate. com* editorial, the election reveals evolving French LGBTQ attitudes and the movement for LGBTQ rights. It's not a monolithic community. Many French gay voters have shifted right. (Estimates are that as many as 20% of US LGBTQ voters voted for President Trump.) The whole phenomena invites the question: What relationship does sexual orientation have to progressive values, here in the US and abroad?

European LGBTQ activists have called out ambitious gay pols who've jumped on board the National Front's ticket at local levels. They've done so, in part, because the Left parties, including the fractured Socialist Party, remain homophobic and slow to support LGBTQ candidates as well as women. As with Trump, the pro-Le Pen LGBTQ vote reflects a rejection of failed establishment political parties.

What to make of US Trump and French Le Pen voters?
I ask the question: Are the polished, French conservative gays vying to be local mayors all racist, fascist, self-hating closet cases? Some may be, but most consider themselves to be socially progressive and fiscally conservative: mainstream Log-Cabin types. US and French conservative gays view their nations' economic malaise and the issue of unchecked immigration and ISIS bombings as more politically urgent than the right to marry or Congress passing a federal anti-discrimination act. In France, as perhaps in the US, they don't know their Muslim and Arab neighbors, they feel alienated in their fast-changing mixed neighborhoods and the world at-large, and they worry about ISIS bombs.

As is often the case, an ostracized group is frequently defined by their oppressors. How they view themselves takes shape as they react to oppression. Perhaps that's what's happening now among LGBTQ groups here and in France.

How have you responded to Trump's election?
The day after Trump was elected president, I started a group in

the Bay Area. We have fifteen hundred members. We put out posters and memes that are quick work bringing attention to various issues.

Since this interview, d'Adesky founded An Anti-Project 2025 Education & Reporting Platform, now operating as Resisting Project 2025.

SALMAN RUSHDIE TACKLES GENDER IDENTITY IN *THE GOLDEN HOUSE*

Salman Rushdie (born 1947) sets his twelfth novel, *The Golden House*, in New York City. The action begins on the day of Barack Obama's first inauguration January 20, 2009. Sadly, on August 12, 2022, Rushdie was stabbed multiple times just as he began a public lecture at the Chautauqua Institution in Chautauqua, New York. He lost one eye as a result of the attack but has since published the novel *Victory City*.

His story opens when the enigmatic, foreign billionaire Nero Golden takes up residence in "the Gardens," a storied gated community in Greenwich Village. With his three sons, Golden ceremoniously arrives to re-establish himself in the U.S. One of Golden's sons struggles with his gender identity and wrestles with the existential choices it implies. The 400-page book, which has been described as part *The Great Gatsby* and part *Bonfire of the Vanities*, tells the story of the American Zeitgeist over the past decade: the birther movement, the Tea Party, the superhero movie, and the insurgence of ruthlessly ambitious, media-savvy villains who wear makeup and have colored hair.

Born in India in 1947, Sir Salman Rushdie was educated

at Cambridge University and came of age in England – he is a knight of the realm – but has lived in New York City for much of his adult life. His fourth novel, *The Satanic Verses*, provoked a fatwa on his life, issued by Iran 's Ayatollah Khomeini in 1989. The pronouncement placed Rushdie in mortal danger for the next decade, and the book's publication was met with demonstrations around the world. Rushdie barely survived that threat; the book became an international bestseller. Even before *Satanic Verses*, Rushdie had won the Booker Prize, in 1981, for *Midnight's Children*. Subsequent books have included novels such as *The Ground Beneath Her Feet* and *The Enchantress of Florence*.

***

What did you hope to achieve with The Golden House?
I wanted to tell a good story that people would enjoy reading. My previous novel was kind of a fairy tale deal, and I thought I would try to write an opposite novel with a large, panoramic view, a social realist novel. That was my starting point.

So that was your use of realism with references to film, the arts and literature?
Yes, I was trying to make a portrait of a particular moment in American life, the last eight years or so. Particularly New York City, just trying to smell what's in the air and respond to it. That was one part. The other part is a story about this crazy family which I've probably had in my head for a while before they'd come to New York. I just brought the two together.

Is Nero Golden a composite?

He comes from the particular background of the Indian super-rich. I know some of those people. Nero is not based on anybody in particular, but he is also not a composite. I don't think it would be right to say he is a composite. He's pretty much himself.

All great cultures have their madmen – Rome, Germany, now the U.S. Is this our post-Cold War dark age?

It has certainly darkened very fast in the last six months or so. I'd actually thought the previous eight years, a lot of them, were a time of considerable optimism. And the changing of that optimism of 2008 to its antithesis in the present is what I was trying to capture (in *The Golden House*).

Your storytelling sense of humor comes through in **The Golden House** *and has made me laugh out loud.*

I'm glad to hear it. I've been trying to persuade people that this novel – my novels – are funny. People have somehow forgotten there is a comic dimension to my writing.

Are you expecting blowback on this book? Did you intend to make the point that the U.S. and our enemies are equally absurd?

I don't know about blowback, though I've had blowback in my time. I don't frankly give much thought to it. I just try to do the thing I have in front of me and hope that people respond to it in the right way.

Does your sense of humor help you survive?

No question. A sense of the absurd and the ridiculous is a great asset in dark times. That certainly has been true in my own dark times. On a daily basis, I'm grateful for the comedians who respond to the situation in the U.S. If it weren't for Stephen Colbert, John Oliver, and Samantha Bee, our days would be a lot bleaker.

A quote about Nero Golden: "This was a powerful man; no, more than that – a man really in love with the idea of himself as powerful." Trump?
I wasn't only thinking of Trump. That's a statement that could be made about many people who are corrupted by power. As the old saying goes: Absolute power corrupts absolutely.

The same can be said of anyone puffed up about himself?
Over the years I've met quite a few extremely powerful people, and the love of power is something I always found extremely unattractive. The most impressive powerful people I've met genuinely see themselves as public servants. They're not obsessed with the idea of themselves as powerful. So, I think there's both kinds of people. Some people respond in a very ethical way to having power. They don't see it as a tool or as an indication of their own glory.

One of the key elements of *Golden* is for me to ask if it's possible for a man to be simultaneously evil and good. That was the kind of character I was trying to build and explore – somebody who was, in one part of his being, guilty of much that is reprehensible or even criminal, and in another part of his being, capable of love and caring, even virtue. But I wanted to see how those qualities co-exist, play out at the same time.

Did Stalin love Svetlana, his daughter?
Well, different kind of animal, but yes. Can you think of somebody who was a good person but who also wasn't capable of things that were extremely bad? To try to show a person who was morally "double" in some way. I wanted to see how I could do that. That was my starting point for Golden's character.

Good men do evil. Evil men do good.
For sure. There's a very funny novella, *The Cloven Viscount*, by Italo Calvino, in which the prodigal character is dissected by a sword on the battlefield. The two halves get sown up individually and survive. One half ends up being incredibly evil and one half ends up being incredibly saintly. And they both do equal amounts of damage. Two halves of the same man. All the virtue ends up in one half and all the bad ends up in the other half, and both are catastrophic.

Regarding the LGBT community in majority-Muslim countries, do gay people represent the "decadent West" who are to be thrown from buildings, stoned, or "honor killed" by family?
There is quite a substantial gay population in the Islamic world. I think there's a lot of prejudice. People in the gay community, and certainly in the transgender community, face real obstacles. Not only in Islamic countries but even here.

I grew up in Bombay, which has always been home to quite a

substantial transgender community, the Hijra. I've spent time in that community listening to their stories and hearing the convictions of their lives. That was for me one of the starting points in writing about an increasingly central subject of gender identity these days. Here in New York, I've had a couple of friends who have transitioned. One in each direction, male to female and female to male. Yes, these are people I care about who've gone through this process. That's been another starting point for me.

Taking those personal elements, I tried to learn as much as I could, to explore as thoroughly as I could. When writing a contemporary novel which tries to take on the present moment, you really have to respond to the stuff that's in the air. LGBT rights are very much in the air. I wanted to respond to that.

In India, this terrible thing happened. Under a previous government (in 2009), homosexuality was legalized, decriminalized. Many gay people came out and they lived normal lives at last. And now this new government came in, and the Indian high court has effectively recriminalized homosexuality (by not recognizing the 2009 decriminalization decision). So that now homosexuality is, once again, illegal in India. Now all those people who came out are, in theory, at risk. That's a very bad situation. Writers have had conversations about and have written about their own sexual orientation. Now they are now asking: can I expect a knock on the door because I am openly gay? I think it's pretty difficult.

Even if a family or friend privately wants to be accepting, the larger culture may impede that gesture?

One of things that I found when doing this work with the transgender community in Bombay is that some of them had families that were accepting. Some had families that were very rejectionist. Some of them had come to Bombay, leaving their families behind, not having their acceptance. Others would go home to their family. As we might expect, there is some of one, some of the other.

Sarah Schulman has made popular the work of Jasbir K. Puar, namely her ideas about homo-nationalism and "pinkwashing."

Yes, I know who Sarah Schulman is. I tried to pick up all the plot dimensions I could. What I was trying to do is make a portrait of a character who had a strong sense that maybe his gender identity either needed re-assigning or had shifted, but who was agonized about it. I wanted somebody for whom it was really difficult to consider that he might need to change his identity. Really, what I was trying to do is to get into that pain, to talk about the pain of people for whom there is no support, for whom there are very contradictory feelings and who are not clear about who they are. They feel there's something wrong with the way in which they present (themselves), but they actually are not clear about who they are and where they wish to go. It was that confusion I wanted to enter into.

That would be the richest way to portray all the elements of that situation?

I hope so. I didn't want to be judgmental or have some kind

of lazy attitude. I think literature at its best is not judgmental. It doesn't tell the reader what to think about what's being portrayed. Literature at its best creates a world that readers enter, in which they can be challenged or provoked but in which they make up their minds about the world they were shown around. That's what I wanted in a novel that deals with aspects of gender identity.

That's one way we might say that literature and journalism intersect?

Yes, I don't really make a big distinction between fiction and nonfiction anymore, because I think some of the work I most admire is nonfiction. I'm teaching a graduate seminar at NYU on the theme of creative nonfiction. I do think the best writing done in the last fifty or sixty years has been highly creative nonfiction, starting with the New Journalism all the way up to Svetlana Alexievich, who won the 2015 Nobel Prize for Literature. I have great admiration for the way journalists make a subject imaginatively creative for the reader. There's a bit of me that wants to do the spadework of a journalist. I want to immerse myself in a subject and know that I know it.

How do you think the LGBT community will fare under President Trump?

It's a very resilient community and it will fight back, but I think it is one of the many (minorities) that will have to fight under this administration. If indeed the administration lasts for four years, which I find difficult to believe – and then I wonder if that's wishful thinking. Like many people, I'm anxious to see what the investigation by Special Counsel Robert Mueller brings up. Also, the rate at which the administration is melting down. It's hard to believe this will go on for four years. Today on social media is a picture of people around President Trump. There's Priebus, Spicer, Flynn. All of them are gone in six months. The only senior member of his staff who is still in the picture is Pence. You begin to wonder if it's the President or Vice President who will go next.

It's like a reality show in real time?
Unfortunately, that's exactly what it's like. Watching America turn into *Celebrity Apprentice*.

What are your immediate fears as an individual?
I'm not particularly afraid of much. You were talking about journalists as well as fiction writers. I do think the attack on the press is a very dangerous thing in a democracy. One of the things we can stand up for in America is a free press. When the most powerful voices in the land set out to undermine the free press and to shake people's confidence in what's presented as the truth, that is historically the first step towards authoritarianism that has been taken by dictators around the world. First you devalue the truth. Then persuade people that they can only get the truth from your mouth. Then you can say anything you want. I worry very much about attacks on the press, on free expression generally, that we have witnessed in the last six months.

What are your immediate fears for the world?

I hope we'll still be here in six months. A friend said to me the other day after only six months of Trump we have people in the streets in America and we're on the brink of nuclear war. I'd like the world to survive. I have children and want them to have a proper life in this world. Having had a long period when it appeared the threat of nuclear war was receding, it seems we're going in the opposite direction. Having been through a long period of wanting to save the planet, we now see a regression of that, in this country, at any rate. All of that is of great concern.

In honor of your sense of humor, your optimism, what are your immediate hopes as an individual?
My short-term hope is that Trump won't last, but I know that only means we get Pence. But, you know, I'll take one asshole at a time. I do place a lot of optimism in the younger generation in this country and around the world. They are much more idealistic, a more environmentally concerned generation, one with a real sense of social justice. They also have energy to stand up to it, to protest, to mobilize, to be activists. It may be that we have to be saved by our children.

DANIEL MENDELSOHN: *THE ODYSSEY* IS ALL ABOUT FATHER AND SON

In *An Odyssey: A Father, a Son, and an Epic*, Daniel Mendelsohn reveals what happened when his 81-year-old father enrolled in his Bard College seminar on *The Odyssey* and their subsequent Greek cruise (their "own little epic"). Mendelsohn also discusses his writing work-style and his 2009 translation of the Greek poet C. V. Cavafy's complete works.

Mendelsohn flies in the face of conventional Freudian theory – that "a hero is a man who stands up manfully against his father and in the end victoriously overcomes him." What Mendelsohn does is far less complicated and emotion-laden. He simply goes on an extended trip with his father. And they bond. Makes you wonder what Freud thought about his own father, Jacob. According to personal accounts, Freud viewed him with ambivalence, a mix of admiration and resentment, often seeing him as a rival for his mother's affection. No rivalries for the Mendelsohns. His mother just doesn't like to travel. No need for complicated psychoanalytical theories. She's a homebody, that's all. *New York Times* reviewer Dwight Garner called it "Rich, vivid, a blood-warm book . . . a deeply moving tale of a father and son's transformative journey in reading – and reliving – the *Odyssey*. What catches you off guard about this memoir is how moving it is: it has many things to say not only about Homer's epic poem, but about fathers and sons."

An accomplished author, reporter, and literary critic, Daniel Mendelsohn has garnered his widest acclaim to date for *The Lost: A Search for Six of Six Million* – the story of his search for the truth behind his family's tragic past in World War II. With 'identity politics' shredded by our last presidential election, readers will find *The Elusive Embrace* "a profound exploration of the mysteries of identity." Mendelsohn examines his own life and its "rich conflictedness of things" as he reflects on "the double lives" led by so many queers while navigating and negotiating their "desire for love" and their "love of desire" and family expectations of homonormativity. Literary critic Hilton Als hailed *Embrace* as "equal to Whitman's 'Song of Myself.'"

Mendelsohn's work, although routinely deep and multifaceted in its considerations, does have a soft underbelly accessible to all.

Your father was a retired research scientist who attended your twelve-week seminar on The Odyssey *at Bard College. Then, you both went on the Odyssey Cruise. Was that your own epic voyage with your father?*

Oh, absolutely. My dad, who was 81, had always wanted to travel. My mother really doesn't like to travel, and being a mid-century Jewish couple, he couldn't imagine doing anything without her. It wasn't until my father was in his seventies that I started going to international literary festivals and bookstores, and I started taking him everywhere. But this trip was obviously special. And it was certainly our own little epic. That's when the book came into focus.

Mom doesn't like to travel?
She's a stay-at-home mom who is very intelligent and well-read. The travel bug never bit her, although my dad would have liked to travel a lot when he was younger. So, I cherished the opportunity to take him along. Basically, the last ten years of his life, wherever I went I took him, and we had a great time. But the Odyssey Cruise was obviously special.

And the parallels are amazing. Both your story and **The Odyssey** *are nonlinear.*
Yes, exactly. When we took the cruise, I wasn't planning on writing a book. When he took my class, I thought maybe I'd get an interesting article out if it: How my octogenarian father took my Odyssey course. It wasn't until we were on the cruise, about halfway through, did I begin to think it might be something bigger. As you point out, the whole experience was very nonlinear. I love moving in circles rather than a straight line. Having my father be part of the experience, first in the classroom and then on the cruise, well, after a certain time I realized what I had.

When did you actually start a notebook?
About halfway through the cruise. We started to have these amazing experiences, like going into Calypso's Cave, or meeting an elderly gentleman with a scar on his thigh just like Odysseus

had. In Book 19, when Odysseus returns home, Eurycea, who had been his nurse, recognizes him by a scar on his thigh. When these things started to occur, I started getting serious.

And you have to remember that I didn't know my father would fall ill and die within six months. Of course, I took a break from everything during the months that he was ill and for a couple of months after he died. When I look back at what turned out to be the last year of his life, I realized there was a narrative arc – the classroom, the cruise, the hospital. That's when I told my agent that this is going to be a book.

Not to reduce your father's memory to a technical term, but you had a through line?
Yes. We're both journalists, so I don't think it's wrong. Sometimes you don't know you have a story until you have a certain vantage point. On the cruise I started running back to the stateroom and typing notes. He would ask: What do you think you'll be doing with this? I'd reply: I don't know but I think it's going to be something. I've written two other family memoirs, so he knew what I'm about. In that way he became approvingly aware of the book as did some inquisitive passengers who knew I'm a writer.

Any Trojan horses? Did you discuss your gayness? What was your first discussion with him?
My father was the original classicist in our family. We were always talking about gayness. Given the culture in which we were immersed, same-sex relations came up often as a topic. He

was totally cool with it. My father was really wonderful when I came out to the entire family. I started out writing for the gay press. My first memoir was very much about that. On the cruise, we hung out with a San Francisco gay couple – a doctor and his partner. One was my dad's age, the other younger. My father adored them, and we spent most of our time with them. I'm very lucky because my parents were always very cool about my being gay.

Your father witnessed a lot of cultural change over the course of his lifetime?
I'd like to think I educated him over the course of my life. I came to realize that my father could be cruel sometimes when he had emotions he didn't know how to express. For him, especially when he was younger, his feelings could come out as anger or disdain or even cruelty if he had worries about his children when we were a young family.

There's a passage in the book about how he treated a gay student when he was in high school – pretty sweetly and gently, actually, and that was the 1940s. But for a Jewish guy from the Bronx of his vintage, he was actually pretty cool about things. It's interesting to look at men of that generation. My dad was born in 1929, and over the course of my life I realized he was quite a gentle person who didn't always know how to express it. My parents didn't bat an eye when I came out in 1980, when it wasn't a given that you'd fare well.

Did your course help him understand homosexuality?

He read many of the Greek classics before taking my course and was always curious about how things worked. He thought it was interesting. He was highly intelligent, and I explained it all to him.

This blending of the personal and the literary is a hallmark of your work, correct?

Like all my other books, this one entwines two kinds of narratives, one personal and one critical or literary. I've done this in all my books now. To me, the most important thing about the experience that led to this book is that even people who haven't read *The Odyssey* know it's about this guy who's been separated from his wife for twenty years and is madly trying to get home so he can be reunited with her. Having read and taught *The Odyssey* many times over, and having had two mentors who were both experts on the manuscript, it wasn't until I had my father in that seminar that I realized the extent to which *The Odyssey* is even more about father and son. People don't think of it as a father–son story, but there's much more real estate devoted to the father–son passages than to the husband–wife situation. How could I not have noticed that before? It's like looking at *The Odyssey* with a special pair of glasses – a father–son pair – because my dad was sitting right there, and suddenly all this stuff about fathers and sons leapt out at me in a way that had never happened before.

Shifting gears a little, Cavafy's poetry also leapt out at you. You've translated all of his work, correct?

Yes, that book is his complete poetry, every aspect of his verse

(*CP Cavafy: The Complete Poems*, 2012). It took me twelve years. At the time I started, around 1994, there were not many good translations. There was one that was the standard, and, although it was very good, I felt there were aspects of Cavafy's poetry that needed to be brought out more, certain formal aspects. For example, some of his poems rhyme, a lot of them are actually sonnets, and you wouldn't have guessed that by reading previous translations. People don't realize that, because it's not something that was emphasized in the standard translations until I started to work on my own.

Earlier translators were heavy-handed in what they removed by de-emphasizing?
But I don't want to dis anyone's translation, like Edmund Keely's work. (Keely was a Princeton professor while Mendelsohn was in graduate school there.) He wanted to bring out the "modernistic" aspects of Cavafy's poetry, since he was a Modern poet, so that's what he emphasized. If you're a translator, you realize that you cannot bring out every aspect of someone's work. You have to choose your battles. Keely's translation was the standard published in the 70s. It really brought out the crispness of Cavafy's work. But I felt that readers needed to know that Cavafy was a 19th- and 20th-century poet who straddled both periods of time. He was interested in forms: sonnets and rhymes. Every translation provokes a response; it's a seesaw effect.

As a gay person, I felt that there were kinds of nuances that I wanted to communicate. For example, there's a Greek word for pleasure, hedone. It's actually connected to our word, hedonistic. It's the same root in ancient Greek. In Keely's translation, he almost always translates that one word as sensual pleasure. Why does he have to call it sensual, to distinguish it from what? Being gay, that would never have occurred to me. When Cavafy is referring to sex between men, you know exactly what he's talking about. I thought he made certain passages a little bit clinical by always referring to male-on-male sex as sensual pleasure. I wanted to de-psychologize it, make it seem more natural. Pleasure is pleasure.

And Cavafy wasn't hiding anything when he wrote it?
No, which is amazing, given that he was writing in the 1890s and into the 1920s. Nothing cagey, no coding, he never pretended. He was always very straightforward about men having sex with men. I wanted to bring out the matter-of-factness about that.

Literary legend says that poets burn brightest when younger, but Cavafy doesn't fit that mold?
Cavafy started writing in his thirties and it wasn't very good. It wasn't until his forties that started producing a succession of masterful work. I think Cavafy got better and better as he got older. He was only seventy when he died. No one would contest that his work just got richer, more pared down, more expressive, more concentrated as he got older. Americans are in love with the idea of the young genius, the early success story. We anoint young writers who come out of the gate with an 800-page bestseller. In reality, most writers get better as they age, because you know more as you get older.

You and Edmund White have sparred in the recent past. It happened in **The New York Review of Books,** *a journal for which you both write. Can you offer any background?*

I reviewed his memoir *City Boy: My Life in New York during the 1960s and 70s* for *New York Review of Books.* I expressed the view that he was really concerned more with the writers he mentioned than with their work. I just thought it was kind of a lazy book. I admire a lot of his early writing, but I thought he was coasting a bit in that book. I just didn't find it very persuasive. Since he is the eminence grise of gay writers, the book should have been better. I think he has been comfortable to be the king of that city. As you become more prominent, you must improve, not rest on your reputation. My question is, did he give up something when he decided to become the king of gay letters? What was lost when he decided to be the big fish in that pond? In my mind, I want to be in the ocean, not the pond.

I don't want to criticize him; I was just reviewing his book. I don't even know him. I met him at a party once twenty years ago at Princeton (where White currently teaches creative writing). My review may reflect a generational thing. White is twenty years older than I am. I came along at a different moment. For his generation, it was so important for gay writers and their work to be recognized. By the time I started writing in the 90s, it wasn't that big a thing for a writer to be gay. Today, gay writers don't have to write about gay things. Being gay now can be secondary to your words. The whole point of being a writer is precisely that you can be liberated to write about whatever you want. With White, I thought he allowed himself to be, chose to be, in a kind of a literary ghetto. It's still important for gay people to be recognized as writers for good writing, not necessarily for being gay. That's very important.

You've said that writers learn from an intelligent reviewer, not necessarily a positive review. What have you learned from intelligent reviews?
You really learn a lot. I really am serious about that as a person who writes books and reviews. Meaningful criticism is beneficial. We all want to be better. No one becomes a creative person for ego gratification. You don't become a writer to win prizes. The point is we all know a writer has to always be doing his best work. When people point things out, you learn.

I think my new book is by far my best book. Many people read my Holocaust book, a family memoir (*The Lost: A Search for Six Million*, 2006). Many people loved that book, and I loved that book too. It was an international bestseller. I tried to do some things stylistically which I would not do now. Some reviews pointed out that I was pushing the envelope a little by my long sentences. I listened to them. I think my writing now is much tighter, less showy in places.

When you're doing an essay, is it like shaking a bottle of soda and then off with the cap for all the fizz?
I do a tremendous amount of research. I was trained as an academic. One mentor said to me: You can't write anything until you've read everything. So, I can take months to write one of the *New Yorker* or *New York Review of Books* essays. I usually try to

read everything that seems to me to be germane. You read all of the works by the author you're writing about and everything all around it – what he read, his influences. I write very fast. All my essay first drafts are complete within a day. I usually wake up at 6 a.m., then start writing at about 7:30 a.m. and go until 6 p.m. It may not be perfect but I like to get everything down. I usually have about 70 to 100 pages of single-spaced notes by the time I start one of those pieces. I've done all the legwork, and then I let it percolate for a few days after I've done all my research. I let it wash over me.

That way you don't have to go back to look up some factoid?
Precisely. And I don't know what an essay's going to be. I never use an outline. Don't know what the ending is going to be. My discovery goes to the very end.

You've been very gracious with your time.
Oh no, this has been so interesting. I wish we could keep going. It's one of the most interesting conversations I've had so far. It's nice to talk about the other work too but I appreciate the way you're trying to see my new book in light of my older work. That's what I try to do when I write about people.

PAINTER DUNCAN HANNAH TALKS ABOUT HIS RAUCOUS LIFE IN 70S NEW YORK CITY

A girlfriend once told Duncan Hannah (1952 – 2022) he slept with a smile on his face. That smile was still there when I talked with him but it is now gone. Hannah died June 11, 2022, of a heart attack while watching a French film.

Among others, Allen Ginsberg made heroic moves on him to no avail. That was Hannah's life in New York City in the raucous '70s. There he was suspended as if in midair somewhere below 14th Street where the gritty underground coursed through the lives of the Max's Kansas City crowd, a place where Fran Lebowitz has said she honed her razor sharp wit.

If it was 'au currant' in 70s NYC, Hannah was there in the moment. He told me over a drink he finds it surprising so many non-New Yorkers don't realize that the during this creative period in the city's popular venues were smallish, they weren't all huge dance halls. "We'd see David Bowie or Rod Stewart in the shadows quietly listening and watching," hoping to divine a trend. His career took him from the sticky floor of CBGB's to the walls of New York's Metropolitan Museum of Art. He was also an actor with an IMDb entry, known for *Christmas, Again* (2014), *The Foreigner* (1978) and *Unmade Beds* (1976).

We recreated our interview – and then some – at the 2018

Milford Writers & Readers Festival when to our surprise some late night denizens from his past haunts were in the room. After our talk, they convened for their own séance. Hannah came across as a survivor with the same joie de vivre from his early years. He unabashedly tells all in *Twentieth-Century Boy: Notebooks of the Seventies*.

~ ᗜᖇ)

It's 1975, you're fresh from Parsons, and you don't miss a thing in New York City. How did you survive?
Well, I could easily have not. So many others didn't.

Why you?
A psychic once told me that I had a guardian angel named Anthony looking after me.

When did you adjust habits?
By 32, I'd given up the party. And I've been very happy to learn since then that the party continues. Life's pretty good for me, but you don't know that when you're in your twenties earnestly discovering yourself.

What drove you then?
It's easy to fall into all the romantic myths about the culture around you. I wanted to be around all those people. Whether that's good or whether that's passion – whatever it is – when you're young, that's a powerful lure.

Your six degrees of separation from Kevin Bacon was ridiculous. And it was pre-internet. How did one manage all those relationships?

Every Wednesday morning you'd grab the *Village Voice*. You got on the telephone. People had their special groups. People let each other know what was happening in the city.

All that was easy for you?

Not really, at least not at first. I was young and not on the guest lists. I had no money. Danny Fields was the one who opened many doors that allowed me to get into many places I normally would not have without him.

So, there you were, a straight kid from Minneapolis, cute as the day is long, mixing in with high-brow, low-brow, straight, gay, sex, drugs, rock and roll. One big social cocktail.

I certainly had people interested in me, some funny stories around all that.

Do tell?

Allen Ginsberg, for example. I always admired his work. When I finally met him, he would always make a play for me, especially early on he made *big* plays for me.

And then what?

I told Ginsberg he was a hero of mine, and all he wanted to do was get in my pants. Why couldn't we be creative together? Why couldn't we be creative peers?

How did that go over?

William Burroughs was there, saw everything, when he put the squeeze on me. Burroughs said, "Finally, Ginsberg, somebody has your number."

How did that eventually play out?

I would run into Ginsberg over and over at various venues throughout the '80s, and even later. And each time I'd see him he hadn't remembered the previous times. But the coda to that story is quite nice. By the '90s he had asked if I would participate in a two person show of his photographs and my paintings. I'm not sure still then, even at that moment, he realized that he had so often hit on me. I did bring it to his attention. I noted to him that it took a long time for him to see me as an artist, not a pickup.

Ginsberg's reaction?

He asked if we could trade works! Of course, I agreed. And we did.

Finally, it was about your work. My experiences in '70s New York City taught me it was about the work, the creative work. Not about wealth, status, velvet ropes. The creative class was accessible.

Yes, it's true. Everyone below 14th Street knew one another. It was a very small group. And it *was* about the work, not about money or fame or fortune. People actually had a sincere interest in what others were doing creatively.

Eventually, their ideas informed the larger public?
For sure. It was an underground. Early into it all we felt we had a shared secret. But nothing stays underground for any length of time. It quickly goes above ground.

One above ground experience in 1980 – the Times Square Show (a seminal group exhibition organized by Collaborative Projects Inc., or Colab, where your work hung alongside Jean-Michel Basquiat and Keith Haring – fueled your eventual trajectory.
The Times Square Show was our version of social realism.

After the Abstract Expressionists had waned and Pop Art was in full vogue?
Yes, like Pop Art relied on real images, we wanted the world to see what New York City was really like – rats, dirty needles, ghettos, poverty, homelessness. It was about 100 artists who wanted to make a statement.

And this was the "old" Times Square, pre-Mayor Rudy Giuliani and Disney?
A drastically different environment back then.

But you were not a Pop Artist?
Hardly. That's the funny thing. My work did not represent the trend then in terms of art. I had been then, and remain, traditional. The *New York Times* reviewer Brett Sokol wrote (April 21, 2016) that back then, as now, I was "steeped in the figurative traditions of his heroes Edward Hopper and Winslow Homer and excited to follow their career footsteps."

About 100 artists from all backgrounds and presentation styles came together to draw attention to the city's underclass?
Exactly. The building we used was abandoned, as were many in old Times Square. We worried that owners and developers would enrich only themselves rather than, at least in some ways, address affordable housing and homelessness.

A '70s version of intersectional?
Yes. The show was a great crossover. I suppose you're right – the word today would be intersectional. As artists we wanted to show the mosaic of human experience that New York City was in those years. Still is, although it's more polarized between rich and poor.

Besides launching you, did the Times Square Show shape you?
I never paint a protest. I find that art that has an agenda is not effective.

Now that will get you a one-month sentence for re-education in activist boot camp.
Oh yes, I guess it will. But once someone told me that art that was beautiful and brought pleasure was not worth it. Imagine that. I guess I'm a little backwards. I'm not that way at all.

Where do your ideas come from? There you were around Warhol, Pop Artists, Keith Haring, yet ever the traditionalist.
You would think my work would be like Warhol's and others since I have spent so much time in and around that crowd. Well, I'm not a very good modern artist in the sense that my life

is not part of my art. I think that Warhol was idea driven. He was always looking for good ideas. I'm more intuitive; I respond to what I love. I see something beautiful, and I want to paint it. That's how I work.

How did you cull from twenty black notebooks what became your book?
When I actually started doing the book, I was discarding three quarters of what I found in the journals. But I was lucky to have written dialogue because dialogue would have been forgotten. Dialogue can take you back to a moment, create a visual in your head.

Were you always a journal keeper?
Yes, but in a way that is different than many. I wanted to write in my journals when I was happy, when I was jubilant, when I was celebrating life. So many people were journaling, still now, only when they are depressed or when they have faced tragedy. I've always been very different in that way.

Are you working on something else? Volume 2?
I do have journals leading up to today, but I feel like with this first book I'm on trial or probation. I was afraid the transgressions and the seediness would come to the top. So far with reviews that hasn't happened. This is the first week (as of March 21, 2018) that the book has been out. As I have been responding to interviews, I realize that people are interested in many aspects of what I write about. I do feel a little exposed, but after all, this was 45 years ago, so I'm sure that it'll all be okay.

From the candidness of Twentieth-Century Boy, you must value openness?

I always admired Edmund White's work in the regard that he always put it all out there. Unlike Paul Bowles, for example, whom I have read and admired. But he missed it in *Without Stopping*, his memoir. He just did not reveal a whole lot. Truman Capote referred to the book as *Without Telling*. For me, for others, it was a moveable feast – that madness on the Hudson.

MICHAEL CARROLL'S *STELLA MARIS AND OTHER KEY WEST STORIES* VICIOUS, SLIPPERY FUN

Cuban fisherman relied on the Key West lighthouse called Stella Maris, Star of the Sea, as their beacon. Now short story enthusiasts can rely on Michael Carroll's *Stella Maris And Other Key West Stories* as their guide to good reading. Carroll's second collection of stories draws from his many visits to Key West, a legendary homosexual gathering space known worldwide for its tolerance. Tennessee Williams and Gore Vidal made frequent visits there in the years before it became a savored destination point.

I was in the island paradise on June 12, 2016, when 29-year-old Omar Mateen shot and killed 49 people and wounded 53 more in a mass shooting at Pulse, a gay nightclub in Orlando, Florida, before Orlando Police officers fatally shot him after a three-hour standoff. I'd been invited there by the Greater Key West Chamber of Commerce to file stories about that year's Pride activities. I joined Hollywood Squares celebrity and two-time Emmy Award-winner Bruce Vilach; Jai Rodriguez, Bravo network's Emmy-winning star of reality show *Queer Eye for the Straight Guy*. Stuart Milk, Harvey Milk's nephew and co-founder of the Harvey Milk Foundation, joined us there.

Padgett Powell says of Carroll's world drawn from his

225

many visits to the most southern point in the US: "Mr. Carroll's world is a little vicious, slippery in its sexuality... strangely reminiscent of the hootier, hard-candy end of the Tennessee Williams spectrum. It is flat-out odd, fun, and seeming true." A Sue Kaufman Prize-winning author, Carroll's end-of-the-line bohemian oasis brings into its pages people from everywhere. Readers are treated to the never-ending parade of condo share tower inhabitants, chain stores, and Redneck Riviera clientele. Key West is a mecca for gay men and the women who love them. John Freeman, *Literary Hub*, calls Carroll "One of the best social observers in American fiction."

⟨⟨⟨ ⟩⟩

Why set the stories in Key West? A favorite place for you?
The long answer is that it hasn't appeared much in recent fiction, but of course there's a long history going back past Ernest Hemingway. Key West needs more coverage to track the changes it's gone through, and pinpoint what, if anything, has endured. Another gay novel, Silas House's *Southernmost*, appeared last year. But other than that, I don't know of much gay coverage of Key West.

The short answer is that it's a place I love, and I go there every year for a month with my husband. This is an incredible privilege, but I don't think I've squandered it. I feel I've soaked up a lot of the place, and that it's unique.

What's Key West like now?

It's a southern town with bohemian values. There are more tourists than ever, but I know how to avoid them if I'm not in the mood for crowds. I spend a lot of time at the Island House. People come from all over the world and say the resort is unique. It's enclosed and complete. Some guys stay there by the pool and at the bar for days at a time. It has a great restaurant. You don't have to leave if you don't want to. Since I've never hooked up on the apps, and am currently not dating anyone, I go there for my annual sex. You can do it in dozens of different places within the confines and do it the way I like best: not on the phone but by first meeting and talking to people. No time-wasting chats. Or you can get into an orgy in somebody's room.

What does the setting allow your characters to do? What does it reveal about them?
You can drink your brains out in the street. You can fuck in public, in the backs of bars, et cetera. In other words, in that setting a writer can reveal a person's true identity and character. And you can bring him in contact with all kinds of other people from around the world. The one thing that persists is that you have to be somewhat open-minded to go to Key West and tolerate its debauchery. You don't move there and expect to have quiet neighbors. You wouldn't call the police on a party.

You're from Florida. Key West is our southern-most point. Are aspects of your stories reflective of your experiences?
I got fascinated by Southern literature young. Truman Capote was my first. But when I write I have to admit I think more about Tennessee Williams. I was flattered by the description.

227

Williams was unafraid. And I don't want to be afraid. I want to be outlandish and absurd and sad and dark. I want to be fun and unexpected.

The title story is based on Williams's novella *The Roman Spring of Mrs. Stone*, where Karen is a disgraced actress, whose husband takes her on a world tour and dies on the plane from Paris to Rome. She stays in Rome and falls in with a louche crowd and falls in love with an impoverished aristocrat.

In my story, Karen dies on the flight down from Ohio and Dale moves into Fantasy House and goes on a fuckfest. He's retired and wealthy so there's nothing holding him back. I trace their past together; she always knew he preferred men. My editor, a woman, made me put back in a finger-fucking flashback I'd taken out thinking it was maybe too much.

Any changes in your writing from the first book to your second book?
My first book still had one of my feet in the narrative-arc form and structure, even though I was attempting to abandon it. The unities of time and place still held slightly, presaging my almost complete abandonment of them in *Stella Maris*. I just got tired of being confined. I wanted the freedom to shift anything I wanted to, setting or point of view or mood or topic. Which really fit for a book on Key West that's heavily populated. One minute in a story you're in one head, then you're in another. You're not supposed to do this. Most of my straight white male friends are appalled or would be if they tried it themselves. But

you know what? Must-see TV and film have changed all the conventions for fiction, as far as I can tell.

Do you still write regularly at your favorite Chelsea bar in New York City?
I wrote three of the stories, the last three, at Barracuda. Then a young guy wanting a mentor came blowing through my life and basically ruined that for me. I don't want to go into the specifics; he's a man I loved, un-sexually, and had great feelings for. But he embarrassed the hell out of me. Not exactly his fault. Some old unresolved issues.

What's important for readers to know about your short stories?
I'm excited for short stories. I love the form because you can endlessly experiment as long as there's good surface tension and some unity of action and character.

One of the stories in *Stella Maris* exemplifies to the extreme my desire to go nuts experimentally. Thematically it is way out there: an unsolved double murder, that never gets solved. Trumpian armies of tourists. And, of course, a character based on me, living in a dry-docked houseboat in the middle of the island. Memories, poetry, sex, outrage, politics, the filth and indignity of being human. That's my sweet spot!

How did all of this go over with your editor?
It takes a great editor who's willing to take chances. I pledged my loyalty and organized most of my own publicity for Ruth Greenstein, because she really didn't have the resources to send

me around the country: she was until recently a one-woman operation. I thought the sex and the feckless structure would daunt her and she'd demand changes. Nope. I bet not a lot of bigger New York publishers would have tolerated my formless meandering and lyrical blathering. It moved me that she was willing to give me a long leash.

What's the state of literature? Gore Vidal often complained that no one reads anymore and that was decades ago.
I don't know where literature is right now, or what its place will be in our culture in the near future, but it takes risk to be any good or in any way influential.

What's next?
I'm writing a dystopian novel set in Fire Island in a Pines collective, with flying motorcycles and vampires and a theocracy and virtual deepfake reality shows. One character, Edmund White, shows up after a long disappearance uploaded into the body of a twenty-something sex worker, and Michael Carroll is paunchy and sixty. (Carroll and White are married.) It is told from different points of view. It began as a novel about my mother, which my wonderful writer friend Xan Price told me I had to finish. I went to Fire Island to pick it up again, on page 55. And soon, it evolved into a dystopia. It's called *Am I Your Lover?* I wrote two hundred-and-something pages this summer, mostly in the Pines

AFTERWORD

Meetings with Remarkable Men (and a Few Women)
by Christopher Bram

Gay literary journalism has a long history of do-it-yourself freelancers. Ever since the days of *One*, the magazine of the Mattachine Society, the most honest writing was done outside the mainstream. For decades straight institutions like the *New York Times* avoided the subject of queer life. Later, when they did write about us, they often got it wrong. In the meantime, however, we had strong, lively, informative writing from other venues: the *Gay Sunshine* interviews, articles in *Fag Rag* and *Christopher Street*, pieces in *The Advocate*, *Gay Community News*, *James White Review* and others. What might be missing in salaries and job stability was made up for with passion, personality, and firsthand experience.

Frank Pizzoli is part of this great tradition of passionate outliers. As he says in his excellent Introduction, he has been writing journalism since he was a kid in central Pennsylvania. He grew up in a village just outside Harrisburg and attended college at nearby Bloomsburg University. Later he founded and ran single-handedly a regional bimonthly alternative newspaper, *The Central Voice*, in his hometown.

His energy is phenomenal. This collection of interviews and reviews from 2007 to 2019, printed in *Lambda Literary Review*, *Windy City Times*, *The Gay and Lesbian Review*, and *The Brooklyn Rail* is just a tip of the iceberg of what he's done as both a writer and an activist.

He is a gifted interviewer. I experienced this firsthand when he interviewed me. He was personable yet professional. He had done his homework, asked excellent questions, then just sat and listened, letting me complete my thoughts. When the interview ran, I recognized all of my ideas, sometimes expressed more clearly than I remembered making them. More important, there were no strange words or proposals I didn't recall sharing. Take it from me, this isn't always the case.

His other interviews and reviews are as deep, persuasive and natural. You often sense laughter in these conversations. Pizzoli is wonderfully flexible. He interviews all three surviving members of the Violet Quill – Edmund White, Andrew Holleran, and Felice Picano – with remarkable ease, although it must've been like herding cats with their different voices. He can hold his own with a dauntingly erudite scholar like Martin Duberman, translating his sometimes dry ideas into emotional truths, especially when they talk about AIDS. And he can be disarming. John Rechy is often a brusque, unhappy man in interviews, but here he is surprisingly amiable, even as he corrects old misconceptions about his work. Maybe Pizzoli caught him on a good day, but I assume he brought out Rechy's better side.

These are all passion pieces, done for love rather than money.

Sometimes passion pieces are written out of hate, but there's no hate here. Pizzoli interviews a couple of writers I dislike, but he manages to bring out their human sides. Sometimes prickly egos appear, but Pizzoli trusts his readers to recognize when a speaker is to be trusted and when they should be doubted. Only occasionally does he ask a follow-up question that signals his skepticism. And he's not afraid to interview, separately, people who are critical of one another. He will even quote one to the other, not to make trouble but simply to extend the conversation. He covers a remarkable range of views: political, aesthetic, radical, liberal, conservative.

There's an enormous amount of gay literary history in this well-orchestrated chorus of voices. It's an oral/choral, literary/social history. Although the interviews and reviews themselves cover just a little over ten years, they look back to World War II and forward to the future. When he cannot talk to the actual horse, as with Gore Vidal and Christopher Isherwood, Pizzoli interviews or reviews the horse's biographers. This collection makes an interesting companion to my own book, *Eminent Outlaws*. His subjects sometimes expand, counter, and even correct points in my literary history. But in the last third of his book Pizzoli enters whole new territory, with more about world politics, gender and things to come. His interview with Anne-christine d'Adesky is first-rate, his conversation with Salman Rushdie a wonderful surprise.

Through these meetings with remarkable men and women, we see the birth of queer literature, its rise and success. We also see its decline due to the changes in the publishing industry and the end of gay and lesbian bookstores. (Gay bookstores were as important to our cause as gay and lesbian bars, places where we shared ideas and information as well as met each other.)

But the literature also lost importance because it was so successful. Queer books were once the only game in town. Our lives could not be discussed anywhere else. But what began in books dispersed into the rest of life: movies, TV shows, political action, law, marriage, talks with family and neighbors. The books were no longer as necessary as they once were.

This is a rare chapter of literary history that's also an important chapter of social and political history. Pizzoli's book is an invaluable record of that chapter. And it is proof that even if the mainstream misunderstands or loses interest in us, there will still be freelance truthtellers like Frank Pizzoli to share the news, good and bad, wherever they can.

ABOUT THE AUTHOR

In 2010, Frank Pizzoli was named a Living Legend as part of Pennsylvania's capital city Harrisburg's sesquicentennial celebrations. His essays, book reviews, profiles, reviews, and interviews with prominent LGBTQ and other authors and celebrities have been published in *LA Weekly, Raw Story, Lambda Literary Review, Windy City Times* (Chicago), *Brooklyn Rail,* abc.com, *Huffington Post, White Crane Review, Instinct, POZ, HIV Plus, AlterNet.com, Body Positive, New York Blade News,* and *Washington Blade,* among many others, and included in the anthologies *Conversations with Edmund White* (University of Kentucky Press), and *Smashing Cathedrals* (ITNA Press). He is the founding publisher and editor of central Pennsylvania's LGBTQ newspaper *The Central Voice,* which in 2018 won second place honors from PA News Media Association for Newspaper of the Year for weekly publications. He is founder of the Pennsylvania-based nonprofit agency Positive Opportunities, Inc., a Points of Light Foundation award winner, that provided employment counseling and training for HIV-positive individuals from 1997 to 2017. His HIV work is cited in *Queering the Countryside: New Frontiers in Rural Queer Studies* (NYU Press) and chronicled in *Out in Central Pennsylvania: The History of an LGBTQ Community* (Penn State University Press, May 2020). In 2020, he was selected for the Legacy Award from Alder Health Services. Pizzoli currently writes for *The Village Voice* and *Pennsylvania Capital-Star.* His work is tracked by MuckRack. In 2024, the LGBT Community Center, Harrisburg, PA, present him with an award for his media and HIV work.

ACKNOWLEDGMENTS

I would like to thank Anne Pizzoli, my read-behind-me eyes, loving brother Joseph Pizzoli who is always in my corner, mother Frances for helping to establish our local library and kindling my love of reading, Agnes Armstrong who never lost faith in this project, electronic file guard Steve Weiland, Steve Leshner for his many helpful comments, Joe and Louise Sukle who have always held doors open for me when others slammed them shut, *Instinct* magazine founder and publisher JR Pratts for his steadfast support, Patrick Merla for his many insights, editor extraordinaire Tom Cardamone, Little Amps and Cornerstone Coffeehouse for the great coffee and warm atmosphere where much of this manuscript took shape, and James Schumacher, my beloved partner and our dog Sherlock who napped at my feet while I worked on the manuscript.

The Library of Homosexual Congress, an imprint of Rebel Satori Press, preserves and promotes classic and provocative works of gay literature and nonfiction, with focuses on the AIDS crisis, the nascent gay rights movement as well as irreverent works of sexual culture and groundbreaking titles that deserve renewed attention.

Curated by Tom Cardamone and Sven Davisson

www.ingramcontent.com/pod-product-compliance
Lightning Source LLC
Chambersburg PA
CBHW022006080426

42733CB00007B/492

* 9 7 8 1 6 0 8 6 4 3 5 9 2 *